DICKENS

GREAT EXPECTATIONS

NOTES

COLES EDITORIAL BOARD

Bound to stay open

Publisher's Note

Otabind (Ota-bind). This book has been bound using the patented Otabind process. You can open this book at any page, gently run your finger down the spine, and the pages will lie flat.

ABOUT COLES NOTES

COLES NOTES have been an indispensible aid to students on five continents since 1948.

COLES NOTES are available for a wide range of individual literary works. Clear, concise explanations and insights are provided along with interesting interpretations and evaluations.

Proper use of COLES NOTES will allow the student to pay greater attention to lectures and spend less time taking notes. This will result in a broader understanding of the work being studied and will free the student for increased participation in discussions.

COLES NOTES are an invaluable aid for review and exam preparation as well as an invitation to explore different interpretive paths.

COLES NOTES are written by experts in their fields. It should be noted that any literary judgement expressed herein is just that – the judgement of one school of thought. Interpretations that diverge from, or totally disagree with any criticism may be equally valid.

COLES NOTES are designed to supplement the text and are not intended as a substitute for reading the text itself. Use of the NOTES will serve not only to clarify the work being studied, but should enhance the readers enjoyment of the topic.

ISBN 0-7740-3302-9

© COPYRIGHT 2003 AND PUBLISHED BY
COLES PUBLISHING COMPANY
TORONTO - CANADA
PRINTED IN CANADA

Manufactured by Webcom Limited
Cover finish: Webcom's Exclusive **DURACOAT**

CONTENTS

Charles Dickens: Life and Works

Charles John Huffam Dickens was born February 7, 1812, in Portsea (now Portsmouth), England. He was the second of eight children born to Elizabeth (Barrow) Dickens and John Dickens, a poorly paid Navy Pay Office clerk. From the age of two to five years, Charles lived in London with his family, where his mother coached him in English and Latin. From the age of six to ten years, the family lived in Chatham, where Charles attended a school run by William Giles, the son of a Baptist minister. In 1823, the family moved to London where Charles spent much time exploring the streets which later became scenes for his novels.

As John Dickens found himself unable to meet his mounting debts (like the immortal Micawber of *David Copperfield*), Elizabeth Dickens attempted to supplement her husband's income by opening a private school for young children—but her efforts were unsuccessful. Charles went to work in a blacking warehouse when he was only 12 years old. Early in 1824, John Dickens was imprisoned for debt at Marshalsea (notoriously portrayed in *Little Dorrit*). Elizabeth Dickens and the six youngest children joined him in the debtors' prison while Charles stayed in a rooming house in London, supporting himself on his shilling-a-day earnings. Dickens described his work in this way:

> It was to cover the pots of paste blacking first with a piece of white paper and then with a piece of blue paper, to tie them round with a string, and then to clip the paper close and neat all round until it looked as smart as a pot of ointment from an apothecary's shop.

He did his work in front of the window and people used to stop and look at him. Dickens hated this and used to shudder with embarrassment. To make matters worse, as in *David Copperfield*, the other boys were rough.

> No words can express the secret agony of my soul, as I sank into this companionship. I worked from morning till night with common men and boys, a shabby child. I know that I tried but ineffectually not to anticipate my money and make it last through the week. I know I have lunged through the streets insufficiently clad and unsatisfactorily fed. I know but for the mercy of God, I might easily have been, for any care that was taken of me, a little robber or a little vagabond.

All this left a deep impression on Dickens' mind and this was reflected in his works. Most of the important child characters in his stories had similarly unpleasant childhoods.

1

While employed at the blacking factory, lodgings of a sort were provided for him. But for the rest, Dickens had to support himself on a very small wage of 6 shillings a week. With no money to go anywhere and little to do, Dickens spent his leisure hours wandering around London, an experience which was to serve him well in the writing of his novels later on. In them, he described not only the imposing places in London, but also the grimy back alleys such as the home of that frightening villain in *Oliver Twist,* Bill Sykes. Dickens acquired a knowledge of London and London life that was second to none, but the blacker side of London life is the more prominent in his novels; the slums in *Bleak House* rather than the fashionable promenades of the West End.

Luckily for Dickens, his father was released from the Marshalsea after six months, after inheriting a legacy enabling him to pay off his debts. Soon after his release, Mr. Dickens quarrelled with the owner of the blacking factory and Charles was dismissed. He went back to school happily, this time to the Wellington Academy at Hampstead. One of his schoolmates said that he was a handsome, curly-headed lad, full of life and fun, and probably was connected with every mischievous prank in the school. During this time he began to write tales which he passed around among the other boys and here, too, he developed a love of amateur theatricals which remained with him all his life, for he was a born actor.

Dickens' love of amateur theatricals led him to arrange private shows for his family and friends. He longed to be a professional actor. He might have fulfilled this ambition later on in his early twenties had not a bad cold prevented him from going to an interview with the stage manager of Covent Garden. At that time, anyway, he had begun to do rather well as a reporter and gave up the idea. But when he left school, at the age of 15, he found himself as a lawyer's clerk, tending to the petty cash ledger.

Dickens' immediate ambition on leaving school changed to that of becoming a reporter, as his father had done on leaving prison. With typical determination, he set out to fit himself for the post, teaching himself shorthand and studying in the evenings at the British Museum. As a result of this, Dickens obtained a job as a shorthand writer in the Courts of Doctors Commons (that is to say, the Law Courts, "Doctors" referring here to Doctors of Law). Here, once again, Dickens was to use his experiences later in his novels. In *A Tale of Two Cities* and *Great Expectations,* the Inns of Court are used, while in *Pickwick Papers* and again in *A Tale of Two Cities,* there are well-known trial scenes. He himself worked in Gray's Inn and it was there that he came to know the ways of lawyers and he speaks of the neighborhood of Chancery as if he knew every stone of its courts and alleys.

When Dickens was 22, he thought it would be more exciting to be a general reporter, and he obtained a job on *The Morning Chronicle* at a salary of 5 guineas a week. He was sent all over the country, from Edinburgh to Exeter. He thoroughly enjoyed every moment of it. As a boy, he'd often gone cold and hungry, but now he could arrive at night at a comfortable hotel, order a good meal, and relax in front of a good fire. But a reporter's life in those days was all not fun and games, for Dickens was a conscientious worker and his work came first.

I have been in my time belated on miry byroads towards the small hours 40 or 50 miles from London in a wheelless carriage with exhausted horses and drunken postboys, and have got back in time for publication, to be received with never-to-be-forgotten compliments by my editor.

It was Dickens' custom to draw his characters from life and place them in situations and surroundings with which he was familiar. In the same way, many of the exciting scenes that are found in the novels spring from Dickens' experiences as a newspaperman. Anyone who's read the descriptions of scenes such as the shipwreck at Yarmouth in *David Copperfield* will realize what a fine reporter he was. This fact did not escape his editors and before long he was being kept in reserve to be sent on important emergency assignments at a moment's notice. His reports, like his novels, had vividness, gusto and a sense of humor, so different from the rather bloodless and factual reports in so many newspapers of the day.

In 1833, Dickens published in the *Monthly Magazine* his first work of fiction, *Dinner at Poplar Walk* (later reprinted as *Mr. Minns and His Cousin*). The following year, Dickens published additional sketches in this journal, as well as in the *Morning Chronicle* and its affiliate, the *Evening Chronicle*. In 1836, all of these short pieces were published together as *Sketches by Boz*. Dickens used the pen name of "Boz" (suggested by his brother's pronunciation of "Moses" while he had a cold). During 1836-37, under the sponsorship of the Chapman and Hall publishing firm, Dickens wrote the serial, *Pickwick Papers*, a humorous, episodic narrative which became widely popular.

Dickens always wrote from experience or deep knowledge of his city. He was a thorough and accurate observer. If he had but a scanty knowledge of his story, he would take great pains to obtain fuller details at first hand. For example, before writing *Nicholas Nickleby*, which was published in 1838, he made sure of his facts by travelling to Yorkshire, where he visited various boarding schools under the pretext of looking for a school for the son of a friend. One school he visited was the Bowes Academy, for he'd read that its headmaster had been in court for cruelty. Here he found the brutal atmosphere that is recaptured in the descriptions of Dotheboys Hall in *Nicholas Nickleby*.

3

In April of 1836, Dickens married Catherine Hogarth, whose father was a music critic and editor of the *Evening Chronicle*. In the late 1830's, Dickens established himself as a social reformer when, as editor of the monthly, *Bentley's Miscellany*, he published *The Mudfrog Papers* and *Oliver Twist* (1837-39). The latter work presented an incriminating picture of the workhouse and the foundling home, thereby attacking the Poor Law and the conduct of charitable institutions. During this period, Dickens was working at a characteristically feverish literary pace, producing such lesser works as *Sketches of Young Gentlemen* (1838) and *Sketches of Young Couples* (1840).

In 1840, Dickens edited the weekly, *Master Humphrey's Clock,* for which he wrote the serials *The Old Curiosity Shop* (1840-41) and *Barnaby Rudge* (1841). Since international copyright regulations were not yet established, Dickens' works were pirated in America. Partially, perhaps out of revenge, he wrote *American Notes* (1842) which contained unfavorable comments on American manners and institutions, and the practice of slavery. Further criticisms were directed at Americans in *Martin Chuzzlewit* (1843-44), a comic satire.

The first of Dickens' Christmas books, *A Christmas Carol*, appeared in 1843, followed by *The Chimes* (1844), *The Cricket on the Hearth* (1845), *The Battle of Life* (1846), and *The Haunted Man* (1848).

From 1844 to 1846, the Dickens family (now grown to five) lived alternately in Italy, Switzerland, and France. Out of this itinerant period came *Pictures from Italy* (1844-45) and *Dombey and Son* (1846-48), which attacked family pride and the worship of wealth. On his return to England in 1847, Dickens organized an amateur theatrical company in which he served as manager and principal actor. In 1851, the group was joined by Wilkie Collins, a prominent playwright and novelist who became Dickens' close friend and collaborator.

David Copperfield (1849-50) reflected a semi-autobiographical account of Dickens' own rise from obscurity to fame. Departing from his earlier farcical caricatures and exaggerations, it marked an artistic advance for the author. In 1850, Dickens and William Henry Wills started *Household Words,* a weekly journal taking a reformist political position. In it appeared *A Child's History of England* (1851-53), *Bleak House* (1852-53), which attacks the chancery courts and the slums around Chancery Lane, and *Little Dorrit* (1855-57), which is a satire of Victorian England.

Dickens' love of acting was one of the great passions of his life. At Christmas in 1853, Dickens gave his first public readings in Birmingham Town Hall, in aid of the establishment of a Birmingham and Midland Institute which would give greater educational opportunities for the working people. There was a natural choice of what to read in *A Christmas Carol.* Dickens wrote to the organizers:

There would be some novelty in the thing as I've never done it in public, though I have in private and, if I may say so, with a great effect on the hearers.

And it was with great effect that he read that night. It was so successful that he was asked to give a second reading three days later. This he consented to do on condition that it should be a working people's night, with cheap seats that working people could afford.

I never saw, nor do I suppose anyone ever did, such a moving sight as the working people's night. There were 2,500 of them there and a more delicately observant audience it is impossible to imagine. They lost nothing, misinterpreted nothing, followed everything closely, laughed and cried with the most delightful correctness.

Dickens frequently visited Birmingham. Once he was there with some friends after a visit to Shakespeare's birthplace at Stratford, and Dr. Johnson's at Lichfield. They stopped longer than expected and ran short of ready cash. They were forced to pawn their gold watches with a Birmingham jeweller. His friends thought this hardly dignified but Dickens could afford to laugh at it. He probably remembered the times as a boy when he had been sent to the pawnshop after dark so that the neighbors would not see, but now with wealth and fame behind him, it was just a huge joke, for who cared who knew?

When he was a boy in Chatham, Dickens had dreamed of buying Gad's Hill Place near Rochester. Once again he was able to fulfill a childhood ambition, for, in 1856, he bought it and lived there most of the time from 1860 until his death.

It gave him a thrill that the house was situated on Shakespeare's Gad's Hill, mentioned in *Henry IV*, Part I. Dickens put up a plaque on the first floor landing:

This house, Gad's Hill Place, stands on the site of Shakespeare's Gad's Hill, ever memorable for its association with Sir John Falstaff in his noble fancy.

Gad's Hill Place was generally full of company, fun and laughter. Later on, Dickens bought the meadow behind the house which he allowed to be used for cricket and other games. A nearby cricket club was allowed to make it their own ground. He also sponsored athletic sports on the meadow for which he provided the prizes. Once again he was successful in his ventures, for one year 2,000 people turned up. Actually, Dickens was not much of a sportsman himself but he was never too busy to help in a good cause.

The joy of Gad's Hill Place was marred for Dickens and his wife by growing marital unhappiness. By 1858, a legal separation was agreed upon and his sister-in-law, Georgina Hogarth, managed Dickens' household affairs from then until his death. Concurrent with the separation, and due to a rift with the part owners of *Household Words,* Dickens and Wills dissolved the periodical and launched in its place, *All the Year Round.* To insure the magazine's success, the first issue began the weekly serial of *A Tale of Two Cities,* followed by other serials including *The Uncommercial Traveller* (1860) which was a commentary on foreign and domestic issues, and *Great Expectations* (1860-61), another semi-autobiographical novel.

Dickens gave public readings from 1859 to 1868 in London, Scotland, and America, which added substantially to his income. His last completed novel was *Our Mutual Friend* (1864-65), another social satire. This was followed by two shorter works published in America by James Thomas Fields: *A Holiday Romance* (1868) which was a children's story, and *George Silverman's Explanation* (1868) which sneers at dissenters.

Back at Gad's Hill Place in 1870, Dickens began work on a suspense tale, *The Mystery of Edwin Drood.* Shortly after completing his sixth instalment, he collapsed in the dining room of his home. He died the following morning, June 9, at the age of 58, and was buried at Westminster Abbey. His request for a simple grave near his last home was ignored.

The characters he created have become personal friends to his many readers through the years. Dickens gave to us a warm, rich and full world, a world such as it is, full of the good and the bad, but always full of hope for the future. He was a man of the ordinary folk. It was about ordinary folk that he wrote and to them he gave the rich world of his imagination.

Introduction to *Great Expectations*

When Dickens began *Great Expectations* in 1860, he was at the height of his maturity as an artist. His personal life, however, was marked by bitterness and unfulfilment. In the late 1850's, his unstable marriage finally collapsed and he began a rather one-sided romance with a young actress, Ellen Ternan, whose coldness is perhaps reflected in the character of Estella in *Great Expectations.* Dickens' radical enthusiasm for social reform had also begun to fade at this point in his life, and was replaced by a sense of frustration and general discontent. After publishing *A Tale of Two Cities,* in which his fascination with the working class and violent revolution is evident, Dickens turned his back on social activism and became involved in writing a series of papers later collected as *The Uncommercial Traveller*. While engaged in these writings, an interesting opportunity opened up for him.

The Irish novelist Charles Lever was publishing a serialized novel, entitled *The Day's Ride* in *All the Year Round*, a family weekly magazine which Dickens edited. Because Lever's novel was so unpopular, the periodical was losing readers, and Dickens decided something must be done to regain support. He had previously decided to write a novel and publish it, as had before been his practice, in monthly parts; however, the falling off in readers gave him the new opportunity. He would plan and publish the novel in weekly instalments. Because he published the novel in this manner, Dickens was not guilty of an earlier habit of beginning a novel in a monthly publication, waiting for the reader response, and then gearing subsequent instalments of the novel to meet the readers' whims. The theatrical endings of monthly instalments were no longer necessary, and he could concentrate on a unified aesthetic work. The result was *Great Expectations*, a novel a third shorter than his normal length and one considerably more unified and free of padding. It appeared in weekly issues of *All the Year Round* from December 1, 1860, to August 3, 1861.

Dickens wrote John Forster, his friend and the author of the standard nineteenth century Dickens biography, and explained the origin of the idea for the novel:

> For a little piece I have been writing — or am writing; for I hope to finish it today — such a very fine, new, and grotesque idea has opened upon me, that I begin to doubt whether I had not better cancel the little paper, and reserve the notion for a book. You shall judge as soon as I get it printed. But it so opens out before *me* that I can see the whole of a serial revolving on it, in a most singular and comic manner.

Forster later recounted Dickens' observation that he chose to publish the novel weekly rather than in twenty monthly issues because he did not wish to commit himself to a project which would require two years. Later letters and conversations reveal that the nucleus of the story was Pip's childhood meeting in the marshes with the convict Magwitch and the reappearance of Magwitch, years later when Pip had become a snob, to reveal himself as the person on whom Pip's expectations were based.

Plot Summary

Pip (Philip Pirrip) is an orphan who has been raised by his shrewish sister and her husband, Joe Gargery, a kind-hearted blacksmith. One bleak Christmas Eve, Pip goes wandering in a church-yard at the edge of the marshes. Suddenly a wild-looking stranger appears and demands that Pip bring him food and a file with which to cut the leg-iron he is wearing. When Pip returns the next day with a pork pie and a file for the stranger (obviously an escaped prisoner), he sees another convict whom he mistakes at first for the man he is going to help. The man Pip helps is later recaptured, but before he is taken away, the convict promises Pip he will someday repay the boy for having assisted him.

Pip is not treated well by his sister, and he grows up receiving limited education from the great aunt of Mr. Wopsle, the parish clerk, and her granddaughter, Biddy. A new opportunity is presented to Pip when he is summoned to Satis House, the home of Miss Havisham, an eccentric and wealthy lady. On the day of her wedding long ago, Miss Havisham's bridegroom jilted her. Since that day, all the clocks in her house have been stopped, she has shut out all daylight from her sight, and she continues to wear her bridal dress, now yellowed with age. During Pip's first visit to Satis House, Miss Havisham has Pip entertain her by playing cards with Estella, a very proud and beautiful girl who considers the boy "common." In the course of Pip's numerous visits to Satis House, Pip meets Mr. Jaggers, a lawyer, a pale young gentleman with whom he fights, and a number of Miss Havisham's money-hungry relatives.

One day Mr. Jaggers informs Pip that an unknown benefactor (whom Pip assumes to be Miss Havisham) has made arrangements to provide him with a gentleman's education to be followed by great expectations. Delighted that he will no longer have to remain apprenticed to Joe in the grim blacksmith shop, Pip eagerly accepts the chance to become a gentleman.

Pip now goes to London to be educated by Mr. Matthew Pocket, a relative of Miss Havisham. Pip becomes a close friend of Mr. Pocket's son, Herbert, who turns out to be the pale young gentleman Pip had once fought with at Miss Havisham's. The two young men live in an apartment together at Barnard's Inn, and they begin to associate with a group of aristocratic young men, among them a boorish fellow named Bentley Drummle.

Pip's new-found status makes him ashamed of his humble background. He begins to neglect his old friends, Joe and Biddy. Even the death of his sister fails to affect him.

Miss Havisham decides to send Estella to London so that the young woman can lead a more social life. Miss Havisham asks Pip to meet Estella when she arrives, and Pip becomes more certain than ever that Miss Havisham is the one who has sent him to London to become a gentleman fit to marry Estella. Although Pip is in love with Estella, she shows no signs of affection for him. Estella attracts many admirers in

London, but she appears to favor Bentley Drummle, the very person Pip finds so repulsive.

On the day of Pip's twenty-third birthday, he receives an unwelcome visitor: the convict he had helped long ago on the marshes. The convict, whose name is Abel Magwitch, has returned to England from a penal colony in New South Wales, and has assumed the name Provis. Although the death penalty awaits Magwitch upon his return to England, he has risked this danger so that he can see Pip again. Magwitch now reveals that he has been Pip's benefactor all along, and that he has used the money he made in New South Wales to finance Pip's rise in social status.

Pip's main preoccupation now becomes the preservation of Magwitch. Knowing the truth behind his rise to fortune makes Pip miserable, yet he is determined not to ignore his debt to Magwitch. What adds to Pip's unhappiness, not long after the reappearance of the convict, is learning that Estella is to marry Dummle. Pip's great expectations are now thoroughly destroyed.

Pip discovers some more interesting information through the revelations of Magwitch and Jaggers. He learns that Magwitch is the father of Estella, and Jaggers' housekeeper, Molly, is her mother. It is also revealed that Compeyson, the unidentified convict Pip once saw on the marshes, is the man whom Miss Havisham was supposed to marry.

Hearing that Compeyson is now in London and scheming to kill Magwitch, Pip arranges with Herbert to help Magwitch escape by boat from England. Compeyson informs the authorities of the escape attempt, and Magwitch is taken prisoner again after a struggle with Compeyson, in which the informer is drowned. Magwitch, sentenced to death, dies in jail before the law can run its course.

Penniless again, Pip becomes ill, and is nursed back to health by faithful Joe, who withdraws to the country when his patient improves. Pip, intending to marry Biddy, finds her married to Joe on the same day that he returns to ask their pardon for his long neglect. He then goes to the East with the firm which he helped Herbert to join.

Eleven years later, Pip returns to England, where he finds Joe and Biddy happy with their son, Pip and little girl. On the ruined site of Satis House he meets Estella, now a widow, and in the moonlight around them he sees "no shadow of another parting from her."

The World of *Great Expectations*

Its Social Milieu

Great Expectations, though published at the height of the Victorian Period (1837-1901), is neither set in that period nor does it reflect many of the prevailing attitudes which characterized the age. With the passing of the 1832 Reform Bill, the vote was given to a large section of the middle class; until then, only the landowning aristocracy had that right. (The question of extending the franchise to the laboring class was not to become an issue for three more decades.) The setting of *Great Expectations* precedes that Reform Bill by two decades. Thus, it is somewhat irrelevant to consider the grimy industrial world which was so much a part of several earlier Dickens novels. *Great Expectations* is set in the Regency Period (1811-1820). This was the age in which the aristocracy exercised its snobbishness to the fullest and still felt that, by maintaining a closely restrictive class barrier, the potential invasions from a lower class becoming increasingly urban could be avoided. Shallow pretention, excessive dress, fashionable clubs, and genteel leisure interests were all the order of the day.

Aristocracy in the Regency Period was not based solely on noble blood. Acceptance by the ruling class quite often rested simply on wealth, so long as it could be demonstrated that one had acquired wealth in a gentlemanly manner. Engaging in busines, thus, did not in itself exclude one from aristocratic ranks, but the nature of the business had to separate one from the lower classes. For example, a wholesale businessman could be considered an aristocrat because of both wealth and influence; a retail businessman, on the other hand, could not.

England was suffering all the problems attending the change from a rural economy to one based on industry: rising population, exploitation of the poor, disease, slums, etc. To make matters worse, in confronting these problems, England was clinging to a system of government which had been devised for a much smaller, non-industrial nation. The social system resembled that of the medieval age: gentleman, tradesman, craftsman, apprentice, journeyman — such was the hierarchy. It is little wonder that the conclusion of the long Napoleonic wars with the consequent debt-ridden government and inflated economy, and the increasing urban population made the last years of the antiquated social system painful ones. The split became clear — and it is this split which appears throughout *Great Expectations* — between those in position and power who wished to protect their own and exclude others, and those without position who aspired to it and were willing to do anything to attain it.

The World Shaped by the Characters

Great Expectations displays two worlds: the one accepted by Pip throughout most of the novel and the one created by him in the concluding chapters. Born an orphan and raised by a domineering sister whose husband is a master craftsman (blacksmith), Pip initially has no expectations. Through Joe's devotion, he is provided with the opportunity to follow the same steps which Joe had followed — that is, apprentice to a craftsman. At first he is satisfied with this world; he anticipates eagerly the day that he will be signed over as Joe's apprentice, and wholeheartedly accepts the desirability of the "larks" Joe says they will have together. During this period, Pip views two other rungs in the social ladder: those of the tradesman, Pumblechook and of the criminal, Magwitch. Pumblechook symbolizes a higher social position which (though Pip notes that his sister bows to Pumblechook's every whim), is made less desirable by the indignation which Pip suffers at his uncle's hand. Magwitch's world of persecution, fear, hunger, and the dreaded prison ships is one so far below Pip's own that he reacts to it with fear and pity, emotions which later become revulsion. In helping Magwitch, Pip steals. His conscience, like that of Huck Finn when he helps the negro Jim, plagues him both because he has committed a moral wrong by stealing, and because he has committed a legal wrong by associating himself with a convict.

Joe accepts his place on the social scale with pride. He is a master craftsman whose pleasure is derived from what he does well with his hands. The fire, the forge, his preference for his work clothes, and his pipe all symbolize his acceptance of his life. Pip's chance to follow Joe in this world is changed by Miss Havisham's first invitation (through Pumblechook) for him to come to Satis House and play with Estella. Miss Havisham is a lady, the daughter of a wholesale brewer. That the brewer-gentleman married and had a son by his cook is of no consequence; his aristocratic position resulted simply from the fact that he was a wholesaler who made money. Ironically, Pip accepts the desirability of this world even though he sees it crumbling before his eyes. The brewery is idle (unlike Joe's forge); the garden is desolate; Miss Havisham is herself a relic of a world in which time has stopped because she could not confront intrusions from another world. From this point, Pip's expectations result from a blind acceptance of the ornamental value (Estella) of Miss Havisham's world.

Jaggers' first approach to Joe and Pip solidifies Pip's belief that the world of Miss Havisham is attainable. He has for the first time — in the interval between Miss Havisham's invitation and Jaggers' approach — come to reject his world. The apprenticeship which had before been a magnificent opportunity now becomes a burden which he must bear. With his wealth and expectations, though they came to him by mere chance, Pip comes to accept Miss Havisham's social standard as the only one in which dignity exists and pride can be taken. Biddy's denial of this, when Pip speaks of "raising" Joe, is neither accepted nor rejected; Pip simply does not understand the premises from which she argues.

Pip accepts the world of Miss Havisham until Magwitch reappears and reveals the source of Pip's wealth. After this, a series of blows challenges Pip's beliefs: Miss Havisham's cruelty, Estella's parentage, Drummle's coarseness. As he begins to reject Miss Havisham's world, he (for the first time) hesitates to accept entirely the premises of any other social level. He creates a world in which the virtues characteristic of Joe and of his own early act of kindness toward Magwitch have meaning. For the first time in the novel, he becomes a true protagonist; that is, he acts rather than allows himself to be acted upon. At the end of the novel, he can offer to Estella himself rather than some ambiguous creature created by circumstance. In joining Herbert's firm as a clerk and working until he attains a partnership, he is not an empire builder; rather, he becomes a self-reliant and honest individual who does well enough to achieve contentment.

Dickens' emphasis in the novel is on the world created by, rather than the world accepted by, an individual. Joe, Magwitch, Estella, and Pip are either orphans or else so neglected as children as to make them virtually orphans. Joe rebels against a father who falls below the potential of the master craftsman. Magwitch lives a life of crime but changes and becomes a wealthy businessman. Estella accepts the hardness of Miss Havisham but, after being broken by a cruel husband, affirms that she has been bent into a better shape. Pip accepts the pretensions of a gentleman; then, after being shattered by Magwitch's appearance, affirms the virtues of Joe and the life which Herbert pursues. In Pip, Dickens does not display the sacredness of the individual and the potential of the self-reliant man as a model of the virtues of a rural and unperturbed life. The reader welcomes the fact that Joe and Biddy marry, for it takes care of Pip's momentary desire to propose marriage to Biddy and to attempt a return to the life he had led before his expectations. Pip's future lies with Herbert, not with Joe, and his reappearance at Satis House and meeting with Estella demonstrate this conclusively.

Chapter Summaries and Commentaries

Stage I of Pip's Great Expectations

CHAPTER 1

Summary

The first person narrator of *Great Expectations* is also the novel's protagonist. He calls himself Pip, he says, because when he was a young child he had been unable to pronounce the name with which he was born, Philip Pirrip. Never having seen either of his parents or photographs of them, his first impressions of their appearance "were unreasonably derived from their tombstones." Pip's most vivid early memory is of standing among the tombstones in a churchyard of his native marsh country. There, "on a memorable raw afternoon towards evening," he is startled by "a fearful man" wearing shackles around his legs and torn and mud-soaked clothes. Frightened, Pip tells the man his name and points to where he lives. The man responds by turning Pip upside down, taking from him a piece of bread, and seating him on a high tombstone while he eats the bread. After Pip tells him that he lives with his sister and blacksmith brother-in-law, Mr. and Mrs. Joe Gargery, the man demands that Pip return next morning to the "old Battery over yonder" and bring a file and "wittles" (food). If Pip fails to return or reports their meeting to any person, the man tells him, "your heart and your liver shall be tore out, roasted and ate." There is a young man far more dangerous who hides with him, the man says, and if Pip fails to return, the young man will "creep his way to him and tear him open" — no matter where he may be. Pip promises to return, is released, and runs. Nevertheless, in fascination he turns to watch the man walk away. To Pip the man looks "as if he were eluding the hands of the dead people" who wished to grab his ankles and pull him into the grave. As the frightened Pip runs home, he can see faintly in the darkness the extinguished beacon by which sailors steer when it is lit, and the gallows on which pirates have been hanged. The man going into the distance appears to his mind as one of those pirates "come to life, and come down, and going back to hook himself up again."

Commentary

The opening chapter is extremely important because it presents Pip, the central consciousness on which we must depend throughout the novel. He is an orphan whose only heritage is that created by his own mind, a mind even at an early age drawn to fanciful images of death and persecution (tombstones, graveyard, gallows, darkness, and shackles). Moreover, the eerie Gothic atmosphere created by physical setting — a marsh country graveyard at twilight — is contrasted with Pip's comic reflections (for example, his conclusion from the shape of letters on his father's gravestone that he had been "a square, stout, dark man, with curly black hair"). The mixture of eerieness and comedy creates a prevailing mood of the grotesque.

Notice how the action in this introductory chapter begins immediately, without detailed preparation. Once we are drawn into the story, the narrative develops smoothly and swiftly. Pip's remark about the blacksmith's occupation, for example, leads very naturally to the convict's demand for the file.

CHAPTER 2

Summary

Pip's sister, Mrs. Joe Gargery, is twenty years older than he is and has gained both self-esteem and the approval of her neighbors by raising her younger brother "by hand." To Pip's young mind, the expression means she has raised him by corporal punishment, and since she also often strikes Joe, Pip assumes he also has been brought up "by hand." Mrs. Joe is forceful and "not a good-looking woman;" Joe is "a mild, good-natured, sweet-tempered, easy-going, foolish, dear fellow — a sort of Hercules in strength, and also in weakness." Pip returns from the graveyard to meet Joe in the kitchen of the house. Joe and Pip are "fellow-sufferers" at the hand of Mrs. Joe; thus confidences between the two have been built. To Pip, Joe is "a larger species of child, and as such no more than my equal." On Pip's return, Joe tells him Mrs. Joe has looked for him a dozen times and has now continued her search with Tickler, a cane with which she deals out punishment. Mrs. Joe enters in a "Ram-page;" she beats Pip and, when he tells her he has been to the graveyard, says that her hard life as his "mother" and as "a blacksmith's wife" will drive her to that graveyard. They sit down for dinner, but Pip is afraid to eat his food because he may have no opportunity to take any other for the man in the marshes. Joe and Pip usually compare the speed of their eating, and Joe — taking note that Pip is not eating — is amazed when he looks away for a moment and then notes that Pip's bread is gone. Joe fears that Pip has "bolted" his food too fast, and when Mrs. Joe makes him confess his fear, his response leads her to scold both of them and to give each a bitter tasting dose of Tar-water. Unpleasant as the medicine is, Pip's situation is complicated by the presence of the bread he has hidden in the leg of his trousers. With the "guilty knowledge that I was going to rob Mrs. Joe," Pip imagines the man and his companion to be outside now demanding the food and refusing to wait until tomorrow.

Because it is Christmas Eve, Pip has to stir the pudding for an hour. The task is made quite difficult by the presence of the food he has hidden in his clothing, until he manages to slip away and deposit the food in his room. He finishes his task, then hears the firing of guns in the marshes. When Pip asks the reason for the firing, he is told that another convict has escaped from the Hulks. Since he does not know the meaning of either "convict" or "hulk," the explanation is unsatisfactory and he annoys Mrs. Joe by continuing his questioning. She replies that "people are put in the Hulks |dismantled ships| because they murder, and because they rob, and forge, and do all sorts of bad; and they always begin by asking questions." Pip goes to bed, believing that his questioning and his stealing have already started him on a road which will end in the Hulks. Fearing the man in the marshes, his sister, and the promise he has made, he sleeps lightly, dreaming that he is floating down the Thames when a pirate in the Hulks asks him to come and be hanged. He wakes early, steals food and drink from the pantry, gets a file from the forge, and runs "for the misty marshes."

Commentary

Almost half of Chapter 2 is devoted to presenting the characters of Mr. and Mrs. Gargery. Joe is characterized as good-hearted, mild-mannered, and harmless. Mrs. Joe, on the other hand, is a domineering and pretentious woman who is outwardly dissatisfied with her place on the social scale. She is characterized by images of sharpness and hardness: "a hard and heavy hand," a "tall and bony physique," a coarse apron having an "impregnable bib" which is "stuck full of pins and needles," the cane which she carries, a way of speaking "sharply," "a trenchant way of cutting" bread and butter, refusal to be polite "unless there was company," and a thimble with which she strikes Pip.

Pip's youth, imagination, guilt, and naïvete are emphasized. The bond between Pip and Joe is also stressed in this chapter. Both of them are the helpless victims of Mrs. Joe's temper.

CHAPTER 3

Summary

The next morning is foggy and damp, "as if some goblin had been crying there all night." To Pip's guilty mind, all objects appear running toward him, and he feels his leg joined to the damp cold "as the iron was riveted to the leg of the man I was running to meet." Confusing his way to the Battery, he stumbles on a man whom he first thinks is the man of his previous encounter. Though the dress is similar and the man is also shackled, he realizes it is not the same man. The new convict, swearing, attempts to strike Pip and then runs off into the mist, leaving Pip to assume he has encountered the young man of whom he had been warned. Pip then goes on to find the right man, who is freezing from his night in the cold marshes. Pip, fearing the man is ill, quickly assures him that he has been faithful to his pledge, that he has come alone and brought food and a file. When Pip suggests the young man may want some of the food, the convict laughs; however, he is shaken when Pip reports he has seen the other convict, dressed similarly and with a bruised face. When Pip informs him that the cannon was fired the night before to warn of an escaped convict, the man says he thought that sound was one of the many he imagined which suggested troops pursuing him. Pip shows him the way the man he encountered earlier that morning had gone, and the convict — "filing at his iron like a madman" — is concerned only with ridding himself of the shackles and going in pursuit. Pip, afraid both of the man and of remaining away from home too long, slips off.

Commentary

Pip's role as the Dickensian hero is more fully developed. Already isolated from family and from any social structure which could offer him great expectations, Pip's guilt now increases his sense of being an outcast. The physical setting itself, shrouded by the marshland fog, offers nothing but confusion to him. Although alienated, the Dickensian hero is characteristically charitable; thus Pip's sympathetic feelings for the convict outweigh his fear.

CHAPTER 4

Summary

When Pip arrives home, his theft has not yet been discovered. Mrs. Joe, busily cleaning the house, relieves Pip's fear by accepting the explanation of his absence — that he has been out to hear carols sung. Playing the martyr, Mrs. Joe only comments that, while she would like to hear carols, her position as "a slave with her apron never off" prevents her from doing so. Mrs. Joe returns to her cleaning, even opening the seldom-used parlor for the Christmas festivities. A good housekeeper, she "had an exquisite art of making her cleanliness more uncomfortable and unacceptable than dirt itself." Mrs. Joe goes to church "vicariously;" that is, Joe and Pip go. Joe's black Sunday clothes never seemed to fit him, and Pip's clothes — according to Mrs. Joe's wishes — were made "like a kind of Reformatory, and on no account to let me have the free use of my limbs."

Pip considers confessing his deed at church. When Pip and Joe return from church, the dinner is prepared and the theft is still undiscovered. The awaited guests arrive: Mr. Wopsle, the clerk at church who has a Roman nose and so much pride in his own voice that he wishes the church pulpit were "thrown open" to competition; Mr. and Mrs. Hubble, he a wheelmaker "of a sawdusty fragrance, with his legs extraordinarily wide apart," and she a "little curly sharp-edged person in sky blue" who "held a conventionally juvenile position because she had married Mr. Hubble;" and Uncle Pumblechook, a moderately well-to-do grain merchant who is Joe's uncle (though Mrs. Joe has "appropriated him" and denies Pip the right to call him uncle), and who has "a mouth like a fish, dull staring eyes, and sandy hair standing upright on his head, so that he looked as if he had just been all but choked, and had that moment come to." As he always does, Uncle Pumblechook brings a bottle of sherry and a bottle of port — for which he accepts the usual thanks from Mrs. Joe. Among this group, Pip would have found himself "in a false position," even if he had not robbed the pantry. He is seated at a corner of the table, not allowed to speak, and must suffer "the Pumblechookian elbow" in his eye while he is given the worst scraps of food. Moreover, he is the subject of most of the conversation. All agree that he should be grateful for his status, and, while glaring at him, Mr. Hubble concludes that lack of gratitude in young persons is the result of their being naturally vicious. Joe tries to comfort Pip — as he has frequently done — by giving him gravy; yet "Joe's station and influence were something feebler (if possible) when there was company, than when there was none." Wopsle, criticizing the sermon of the day, discusses "what kind of sermon *he* would have given them" *if* the church pulpit had been "thrown open;" he illustrates by condemning greed and gluttony while glaring at Pip. Pumblechook further belittles Pip by referring to the potential fate from which he was saved by the kindness of Mrs. Joe. So pleasing to Mrs. Joe is this compliment that she offers Pumblechook brandy. Pip is frightened now because he had earlier stolen some brandy to take to the convict, and he had refilled the brandy container with Tar-water; thus Pumblechook runs from the room coughing. Finding comfort in the fact that he is not accused, Pip is again thrown into panic when Mrs. Joe goes for a serving of pork pie. Realizing discovery of the theft is inevitable, Pip can "bear no more" and he runs for his life. At the door he meets a party of soldiers carrying muskets and handcuffs. He imagines they are about to arrest him.

Commentary

The boundaries of Pip's isolation are here enlarged. The reader notes that Mrs. Joe is not unique in her treatment of Pip; rather, this treatment is approved by each layer of society represented by the Christmas guests. Only Joe, whose sympathetic passing of the gravy at Pip's moments of greatest distress establishes a bond of brotherhood, refrains from abusing Pip. One of Pip's great moments of recognition comes in his statement: "I was always treated as if I had insisted on being born in opposition to the dictates of reason, religion, and morality, and against the dissuading arguments of my best friends."

CHAPTER 5

Summary

Because of the sudden appearance of the soldiers, the missing pie is forgotten. The soldiers have come for the services of the blacksmith, and a young sergeant requests that Joe immediately repair a set of handcuffs. Joe finds that the task will require nearly two hours, during which time the company finds that the reason for the urgent request is that the soldiers are under orders to arrest the two escaped convicts in the marshes. Pumblechook offers the wine which he had brought as a gift, and he further gives in to the sergeant's flattery by pouring practically all the two bottles simply for the "credit of handing it about." Pip remarks that the idea of pursuit of the fugitives has added to the company a dessert-like enjoyment which had not existed before the soldiers' arrival. To him the murky shadows from the forge fire seem to shake at the convicts in menace and the pale afternoon almost seems "to have turned pale on their account, poor wretches." Joe finishes his job, and he, Pip, and Mr. Wopsle decide to accompany the soldiers in the pursuit — a decision to which Mrs. Joe agrees only because of her curiosity.

Joe and Pip follow the soldiers, whispering to each other that they hope the search will be unsuccessful. The east wind brings bitter sleet, and Pip (now riding on Joe's shoulders) hopes the sight of him will not lead the convicts to conclude that he has betrayed them to the soldiers. A long shout halts the company as they approach the old Battery; it is soon followed by other shouts, and as the group quickly pursues the sounds, they are able to make out one voice shouting "Murder!" and another "Convicts! Runaways! Guard! This way for the runaway convicts!" The two convicts are found swearing and fighting at the bottom of a ditch. Pip's convict asks the soldiers to note that it was he who called the alarm, saying of his fellow culprit: "I give him up to you! Mind that!" The other convict, unable to speak until they are separately handcuffed, says that Pip's convict had tried to murder him. The soldiers are indifferent to both claims, but it becomes clear that Pip's convict could have escaped had he not, after finding the other "gentleman" convict had followed his example in escaping the Hulks, chosen to bring about their mutual arrest. Pip's convict says he could not let his fellow culprit make a tool of him "afresh and again," and he denies that he attempted murder. Suddenly Pip's convict sees him; Pip slightly moves his hands and shakes his head to indicate he has had nothing to do with the capture. The convict's return look is not understood by Pip, though he notes its attentiveness. Then, carrying red torches in the night, the group moves through the marsh toward the Hulks. The convict never again looks at Pip, but when he reaches the guard's house he asks to make a confession: that he stole the food from the blacksmith. When told that Joe is the blacksmith, he apologizes for the act. Joe replies that he does not know why the man is a convict but that such a "poor miserable fellow-creatur" was welcome to the food. When the convict turns away, Pip hears a sob in his throat. Seeing him board the prison ship, Pip feels as if "it were all over" with the convict.

Commentary

To make the subsequent plot line completely realistic, Dickens here clears up any ambiguity concerning Pip's feeling for his convict. Though Pip had genuinely feared the threat to his "heart and liver," he had actually gained from the encounter an opportunity to bring to the surface elements of human sympathy and feeling which his social situation — dominated by the sheer force of Mrs. Joe and the falsity of the other dinner guests — had forced to remain hidden. Moreover, Pip had (as the subsequent plot of the novel will show) been able to demonstrate that humanity visibly to the captured convict. Joe, who shares Pip's helplessness around Mrs. Joe, is here in a comparable position, for he too regrets the successful capture and willingly forgives the convict's supposed theft. Their mutual humanity causes the apparently doomed convict to sob.

CHAPTER 6

Summary

Before the trip home from the prison-ship has progressed far, Pip becomes sleepy and Joe again carries him. Arriving at home groggy, Pip is quickly awakened by a lecture from Mrs. Joe. He then hears Joe telling of the convict's confession, in response to which the visitors — especially Mr. Pumblechook — hypothesize elaborately on how the convict maneuvered the theft. Again falling asleep, Pip is roughly assisted to bed by Mrs. Joe. Thinking of his unexpected release from guilt, Pip does not recall "any tenderness of conscience in reference to Mrs. Joe," though the fear of being found out is removed. But he does love Joe, "perhaps for no better reason in those early days than because the dear fellow" permitted that love. Though he is tempted to tell Joe the truth, especially when Joe searches for his file, Pip keeps quiet for fear of losing Joe's confidence. Thus, reflecting on his unworldly youth, Pip concludes: "In a word, I was too cowardly to do what I knew to be right, as I had been too cowardly to avoid doing what I knew to be wrong."

Commentary

Pip, alienated from all except Joe, is unwilling to build any barrier which may alter that relationship, even though, first, the potential barrier would merely consist of telling the truth and, second, Joe's previously demonstrated character would suggest that no barrier at all would be built by such a confession. For the first time, Pip has experienced guilt and fear, and he responds with a lack of moral courage that is significant in view of how he will behave later in the novel.

CHAPTER 7

Summary

The events related in the previous chapter take place at a time when Pip's education is quite elementary. Because he is not yet old enough to be apprenticed to Joe, he works as an "odd-boy about the forge" and at any small job which one of the neighbors might have available; these jobs (according to Mrs. Joe) keep him from becoming "Pompeyed |pampered|," and Mrs. Joe makes it known that any earnings must be deposited in a money box from which Pip has no liberty to draw. Each evening he goes to school from six to seven at the cottage of Mr. Wopsle's great-aunt, an old woman who sleeps through each lesson and who is equally incapable of running a little general shop during the day. Most of the real teaching is done by Biddy, a distant relative of Mr. Wopsle. She is an orphan who has "been brought up by hand." Through Biddy's help, Pip becomes somewhat literate which (when demonstrated to Joe) is received "as a miracle of erudition." Joe is illiterate, and he only recognizes the letters of his own name. When Pip questions Joe concerning the reason for his lack of knowledge, he receives the story of Joe's youth. Joe's father, a blacksmith who infrequently devoted himself to his work, beat both Joe's mother and the boy himself. A drunkard, he would pursue his family whenever they tried to run away from him. The good-natured Joe still maintains that his father was a good man, though the latter's failure to provide had forced his son to leave school early and devote himself to the life of a blacksmith. The death of Joe's father in an epileptic fit was soon followed by the death of his mother. Left alone and becoming lonely, Joe met Pip's sister, a "fine figure of a woman" whose boniness and red skin were quite unimportant to Joe when compared to the reputation she had gained for bringing up her young orphan brother "by hand." Pip was then a baby, and Joe had insisted in his proposal of marriage that the baby also join his household at the forge. At the conclusion of Joe's story, Pip breaks "out crying and begging pardon," to which Joe replies: "Ever the best of friends; ain't us, Pip?"

Pip then suggests that he become Joe's teacher; Joe agrees, but warns that the teaching must be done without Mrs. Joe's knowledge — for she "in partickler would not be over partial to my being a scholar, for fear as I might rise." Joe admits that his wife is a "Buster" who is "given to government" and to make known that he endures her behavior because the harsh treatment of his mother has made him "dead afeerd of going wrong in the way of not doing what's right by a woman." Pip discovers "a new admiration of Joe from that night." After their conversation, Joe and Pip prepare for the return of Mrs. Joe, who has been away helping the bachelor Pumblechook on market day. Mrs. Joe arrives, bringing news that Pip is invited next day to play at the house of Miss Havisham, "an immensely rich and grim lady who lived in a large and dismal house barricaded against robbers, and who led a life of seclusion." Pumblechook, a tenant of Miss Havisham's, had gone there to pay the rent and was then asked to find a boy to play at the house. He chose Pip and feels that "this boy's fortune may be made by his going to Miss Havisham's." Pip is to spend the present night at the home of Pumblechook, who will take him next morning to Miss Havisham's. Mrs. Joe scrubs Pip harshly and dresses him in very uncomfortable clothes; thus Pip leaves Joe for the first time, accompanied by Pumblechook who characteristically warns him to "be forever grateful to all friends, but especially unto them which brought you up by hand!" Pip has no idea what to expect of the next day.

Commentary

Significantly, Pip's first parting from Joe falls close on the time of the "new admiration" he has gained for the blacksmith. Succeeding chapters will demonstrate the shallowness of that admiration; thus it is fitting that Dickens in this chapter presents a clear opposition between what is pompous and false (Mr. Wopsle and his great-aunt's school) and those emotions more true and secure — though perhaps less sophisticated (Joe). Though Pip does not know what to expect, he is clearly being prepared by Dickens for a choice later in life.

CHAPTER 8

Summary

Pip spends the night at Pumblechook's (sleeping in the attic), and the next morning he views his uncle's seed store and the businesses which surround it, noting that the watchmaker "seemed to be about the only person in the High Street whose trade engaged his attention." While eating his meager breakfast, Pip is subjected to a conversation consisting of nothing but questions relating to arithmetic, since Pumblechook believes, like Mrs. Joe, that "a mortifying and penitential character" should be included in the diet. At ten o'clock Pip and Pumblechook journey to Miss Havisham's and there see a house "which was of old brick, and dismal, and had a great many bars to it. Some of the windows had been walled up; of those that remained, all the lower were rustily barred." They wait for the bell to be answered and meanwhile view to the side an old and long-abandoned brewery. Answering the door is a "young lady, who was very pretty, and seemed very proud;" she dismisses a disappointed and curious Pumblechook and then leads Pip through the cold courtyard, telling him that the name of the house (Satis) means "that whoever had this house could want nothing else." She is Pip's age but looks much older, self-possessed, and scornful of him. Leading him through dark hallways, she then leaves him at the door of Miss Havisham's room. The room is large and lighted completely by candles. Its most prominent feature is a draped dressing table with a gilded mirror. Miss Havisham herself is dressed totally in clothing that was originally white but is now faded and yellow with age: "the bride within the bridal dress had withered like the dress, and like the flowers, and had no brightness left but the brightness of her sunken eyes." Pip notes that both her watch and a clock in the room are stopped at twenty minutes before nine. Miss Havisham tells him that her heart is broken and she wishes entertainment; thus she commands him: "Play." When he answers that the strange melancholy of the room makes it difficult to carry out her request, she summons the proud girl (Estella), who objects to playing cards with "a common labouring-boy." Though it seems unlikely, Pip thinks he hears Miss Havisham reply to her: "Well? You can break his heart." Estella's contempt for him is "infectious;" he himself begins to despise his coarse hands and to accept as accurate her criticism of him as "a stupid, clumsy labouring-boy." To Miss Havisham's questioning (after he has been hopelessly beaten at cards), Pip says of Estella that she is proud, pretty, insulting, and that he "should like to go home." He is to return in six days, and as Estella leads him through the darkness he wishes "Joe had been rather more genteely brought up, and then |he| should have been so too." Feeling "humiliated, hurt, spurned, offended, angry, sorry," he is given food by Estella as if he "were a dog in disgrace." When tears come to his eyes she leaves, after looking at him "with a quick delight in having been the cause of them." He then cries bitterly, seeing in his treatment a further example of "a perpetual conflict with injustice" which has plagued him since babyhood. After eating, he collects himself and views the decayed brewery and its surroundings. Walking on the brewery casks, he sees Estella far away also walking on them; she then disappears and climbs some stairs; then "a strange thing happened to |his| fancy." He thinks he sees the yellowed figure of Miss Havisham hanging by the neck from a great wooden beam. Soon Estella returns with keys to let him out; she teases him for crying and then dismisses him. Despising himself, Pip thinks: "I was much more ignorant than I had considered myself last night, and generally . . . I was in a low-lived bad way."

Commentary

Pip's innocence is sacrificed in this first visit to Satis House. In accepting Estella's judgment of him, he must not only condemn himself but also the environment (symbolized by Joe and the forge) which has made him what he is. Since he cannot change his environment, he must adopt a false front — and many of the succeeding chapters depict that false front.

Pip's conscious reaction to the scene is one of passive acceptance; his unconscious reaction is aggressively hostile, for in seeing Miss Havisham and sensing that she is the actual author of Estella's unkindness, he sees, in a hallucination, her death by hanging. The reader should attempt to explain this vision and its recurrence in terms of Pip's later heroism, when he saves Miss Havisham from death in the fire.

CHAPTER 9

Summary

Arriving at home, Pip avoids the many questions directed to him by Mrs. Joe and Pumblechook, and he decides — since the truth would probably not be believed — that he will construct an elaborate lie. In this account Miss Havisham is tall, dark, and sits in her room in a black velvet coach while Estella hands her cake and wine through a coach window. All eat cake and wine on gold plates and four dogs are fed veal cutlets out of a silver basket. Mr. Pumblechook, who has never seen Miss Havisham, joins Mrs. Joe in assuming that the account is accurate. When Pip sees Joe in helpless amazement as the tale is told to him, he becomes regretful — but only toward Joe. He later finds Joe in the forge and confesses his lie, telling him of the true humiliation which he felt. Joe can understand neither the cause for the lie nor for Pip's feeling himself inferior, since in his eyes Pip is a fine scholar. Of the lie, he says: "If you can't get to be oncommon through going straight, you'll never get to do it through going crooked." He further adds that it would perhaps be best for common people to play with their own kind, rather than desire the uncommon. Pip goes to bed, romanticizing his place in the events of the day and thinking "how common Estella would consider Joe, a mere blacksmith."

Commentary

Again in this chapter we see Pip's vivid imagination at work as he constructs an elaborate lie about his visit to Miss Havisham's. Ironically, the extraordinary tale he tells his family is no more unbelievable than the truth itself would have been, but Pip chooses to lie since he feels that truth would be stranger than fiction.

It is significant that Pip's conscience is uneasy after lying to Joe. Although Joe soundly advises Pip to be content with truth, to go "straight" rather than "crooked," Pip does not seem deeply impressed with Joe's simple wisdom. Later in the novel, the extent of Pip's departure from the truth and the teachings of Joe will become more evident.

CHAPTER 10

Summary

Pip immediately takes steps to become less common. At evening school, he tells Biddy that he has "a particular reason for wishing to get on in life" and he wishes her to teach him as much as possible. She immediately agrees, but it becomes obvious that the school is not the place for a serious student. After school Pip meets Joe at the Three Jolly Bargemen, a local tavern from which they plan to walk home together. Joe is seated with Mr. Wopsle and "a secret-looking man" who buys drinks for everyone and directs the conversation to the marshes, finally drawing out of Joe an account of the earlier search for the convicts. All during the account, the stranger looks only at Pip and, after making sure of Pip's identity, proceeds to stir his drink *"with a file."* Aware that the man knows his convict, Pip is spellbound, and when he and Joe leave, the stranger hands him some change wrapped in two one-pound notes. Joe, finding at home that the notes cover the coins, considers that a mistake has been made. He returns to the tavern, but the man has disappeared (as Pip suspected). Mrs. Joe puts the notes in an ornamental teapot where "they remained a nightmare to |Pip| many and many a night and day." In bed Pip sleeps badly, thinking "of the guiltily coarse and common thing it was, to be on secret terms of conspiracy with convicts."

Commentary

The effect of Satis House on Pip is made clear in this chapter. As a young boy, his conscience had tormented him for having stolen food from Mrs. Joe. Now his concern is not the theft, a moral offense and crime, but that he has contaminated himself by doing a "coarse and common thing." His self-assumed pretence now blinds him to the human instincts which had led him in innocence to commit an act of charity.

This chapter is also important, as it recalls the convict theme. Pip's nightmare of the reappearance of the file has come true, and will come true again at the crisis.

CHAPTER 11

Summary

At the appointed time Pip returns to Miss Havisham's. Met by Estella, he notes her indifference as she leads him by candlelight through the opposite side of the house. Finding himself in a paved court-yard, he sees a detached house which has as its most prominent feature a clock also stopped at twenty before nine. Estella leads him into a room and tells him to wait with some other people. He is conscious that his coming has interrupted the people's conversation. The three women and one gentleman "somehow conveyed to |Pip| that they were all toadies and humbugs, but that each of them pretended not to know that the others were toadies and humbugs." Their conversation concerns someone named Matthew — obviously a relative whose sense of pro-priety does not meet with their approval. When a bell rings, Estella calls Pip and they leave the room; their exit receives the indignant stares and remarks of the other people. Walking through the corridor, Estella asks Pip if he thinks her pretty and insulting; his answer leads her to slap his face with all her strength, to call him a "little coarse monster," and to provoke him to cry again. Although he is crying inwardly, he says: "I'll never cry for you again."

As they go up the stairs, they meet "a burly man of an exceedingly dark complexion." Though Pip does not know the man will become a part of his life, he does observe the man's appearance closely. The man, smelling of scented soap, takes Pip's chin in his hand, comments that his experiences with boys have taught him that all are "a bad sort of fellows," and warns Pip to behave himself. Estella leaves Pip standing at Miss Havisham's door, and he notes that nothing has changed. When Pip does not seem eager to play, Miss Havisham suggests that he work, and sends him to a room across the hall. The atmosphere of the room reminds him of a marsh mist: "every discernible thing in |the room| was covered with dust and mould, and dropping to pieces." A long center table is covered with a tablecloth "as if a feast had been in preparation when the house and the clocks all stopped together." A centerpiece covered with cobwebs has the appearance of a black fungus growing on the yellow expanse, and "speckled-legged spiders with blotchy bodies" run about. Miss Havisham says that after death she will be laid on that table and people will come and look at her there. The mound of cobwebs in the middle had been her bridal cake. Pip is asked to support her in walking slowly around the table; meanwhile, Estella is summoned and brings the other guests to watch the proceedings. Pip is embarrassed at their presence, but Miss Havisham treats them with contempt. The one called Camilla suggests her concern for Miss Havisham. Miss Havisham immediately attacks this suggestion and this prompts Camilla's tears and an angry remark concerning the person named Matthew. Pip and Miss Havisham continue circling the table while Camilla and Miss Sarah Pocket talk, but when the name Matthew is again mentioned they halt. Miss Havisham says Matthew will stand at her head when she is laid dead upon the table and further tells the others where to stand, saying: "Now you all know where to take your stations when you come to feast upon me." She then dismisses them and continues with Pip to walk around the table. She tells Pip today is her birthday (though she doesn't allow the others to speak of it) and the day on which she was supposed to have been married; she hopes (when the ruin is complete) that she will die on this day. Estella returns and they all go to the other room where he and Estella, who now does not speak, play cards. Then, when the game is over, he is taken down to eat "in the former dog-like manner" — though not before Miss Havisham accents Estella's beauty by trying her jewels on Estella's breast and hair. After eating, Pip is alone and wanders about the decaying garden. Suddenly he meets "a pale young gentleman with red eyelids and light hair." He is about Pip's age, though larger, and he immediately challenges Pip to a fight. Pip, to his great surprise, easily defeats his adversary, and they part in a friendly manner. In the courtyard Estella awaits him "with a bright flush upon her face, as though something had happened to delight her." She allows him to kiss her cheek, but he feels the kiss was given "to the coarse common boy as a piece of money might have been, and that it was worth nothing." Pip returns home.

Commentary

Mention is made of a cousin, Matthew Pocket, by Miss Havisham's relatives. It is he who later directs Pip's education. The "pale young gentleman" that fights with Pip will later be revealed as Herbert Pocket, Matthew's son and eventually a close friend of Pip.

25

CHAPTER 12

Summary

For the next few days, Pip thinks of the fight at Satis House and regrets having beaten his adversary so savagely. He feels sure revenge will be forthcoming, and when the day comes for his return to Satis House his "terrors reached their height." However, his fear proves to be unwarranted, since nothing is said of the fight. Miss Havisham has acquired a wheelchair, and it is Pip's duty to wheel her about the house for several hours at a time, a duty which it is decided he will fulfil on alternate days for the next eight or ten months. Pip tells of his plans to be apprenticed to Joe and, speaking of his desire to better his education, hopes that Miss Havisham "might offer some help towards that desirable end." However, she does not and seems to prefer his remaining ignorant. Of Estella, he remarks: "Sometimes, she would coldly tolerate me; sometimes, she would condescend to me; sometimes, she would be quite familiar with me; sometimes, she would tell me energetically that she hated me." Miss Havisham would often ask his reaction to Estella; she would also display a "miserly relish of Estella's moods" and at times would whisper to her: "Break their hearts, my pride and hope, break their hearts and have no mercy." During these months he wheels Miss Havisham, often singing a blacksmith's song to her. Each time he returns home from Satis House he becomes less and less willing to discuss his experiences. Only to Biddy does he confide, and when Pumblechook (now putting on airs as the originator of the boy's good fortune) and Mrs. Joe discuss his prospects with Miss Havisham, Pip notes that Joe becomes sad. Finally, however, Miss Havisham asks Pip to bring Joe to her with the papers which will make Pip his apprentice. Mrs. Joe, because she is not invited, goes "on the Rampage."

Commentary

Dickens foreshortens time in this chapter so that the reader may view Pip's developing sense of his role and prospects in Satis House. Moreover, we are aware that Pip is suffering from numerous illusions which he has half hidden from himself. While he becomes quiet when Mrs. Joe and Pumblechook discuss his prospects, he obviously does have the idea that some prospects are in store for him. Pip's false front not only alters him in the view of those around him; it also distorts his own perception of his identity.

CHAPTER 13

Summary

Though Joe looks "far better in his working dress," he puts on his Sunday suit and joins Pip for the trip to Miss Havisham's. Mrs. Joe, who decides to spend the time at Pumblechook's, accompanies them part of the way, and she carries with her "articles of property — much as Cleopatra or any other sovereign lady on the Rampage might exhibit her wealth in a pageant or procession." Estella opens the door for Pip and Joe and leads them to Miss Havisham where Joe (because of embarrassment) aggravates Pip by addressing him rather than Miss Havisham when she asks questions. Pip is quite embarrassed by Joe's behavior as they all discuss his apprenticeship — especially when Joe says that their relationship as master and apprentice is "calc'lated to lead to larks" and that Pip is quite happy with the arrangement. When Pip sees that Estella's "eyes laughed mischievously," he is even more embarrassed. Miss Havisham, glancing at Joe "as if she understood what he really was" in spite of his behavior, gives him the premium (twenty-five guineas) which Pip has earned and, after thanks are received, tells Pip that Gargery is his master now and that he is not again to return to Satis House. Joe's only response after leaving the house is that the interview was "astonishing." They return to Pumblechook's where Joe willingly tells his wife two lies: first, that Miss Havisham sends her regrets that her health did not warrant including Mrs. Joe in the invitation, and, second, that the money was sent as a gift to Mrs. Gargery. Pumblechook, "that basest of swindlers," acts as if he had known what would happen, and he accompanies them in his most supreme manner to the magistrates where Pip is to be legally bound as Joe's apprentice. After the churchlike ceremony, they go to the Blue Boar for dinner, and Pumblechook makes the affair more uncomfortable for Pip by constantly referring to the grave significance of an apprentice's papers. Finally they return home, and Pip (feeling "truly wretched") goes to his bedroom and thinks: "[I] had a strong conviction on me that I should never like Joe's trade. I had liked it once, but once was not now."

Commentary

The basic opposition in Pip's character is made evident in this chapter. He is firmly attached to the world of Satis House, especially Estella, by his expectations and by his potential snobbery — a previously hidden characteristic which comes to the surface in his shame at Joe's behavior. Moreover, he is connected to the house in the marshes not (as before) by a simple loyalty to the goodness of Biddy and Joe; rather, he is legally bound by an apprentice system over which his preferences have no power. It is this which makes Pumblechook's remarks at the Blue Boar so painful to him.

CHAPTER 14

Summary

Though Mrs. Joe had always made home rather unpleasant for Pip, "Joe had sanctified it, and |Pip| believed in it." The forge had been to him "the glowing road to manhood and independence." Yet, within a single year (the time of his visits to Satis House), Pip has come to the conclusion that "it is a most miserable thing to feel ashamed of home." Though he does not admit his feelings to the industrious Joe, his life, like the marshes, stretches before him "heavy and blank." Because of the faithful Joe, he never runs away to become a soldier or sailor, and he comments: "I know right well that any good that intermixed itself with my apprenticeship came of plain contented Joe, and not of restless, aspiring, discontented me." Not knowing what he wants, Pip fears that unexpectedly Estella will appear and view him standing "with a black face and hands, doing the coarsest part of |his| work" and will triumph over and despise him. After such thoughts, his home and meals appear more common and he is "more ashamed of home than ever, in |his| own ungracious breast."

Commentary

It is ironic that Pumblechook, Wopsle, and Mrs. Joe have always reminded Pip to "be grateful." In respect to Joe (who has sacrificed for him), Pip has certainly not taken that advice. Increasing self-pity is the most obvious result of his endless tendency to use Estella, Miss Havisham, and Satis House as a standard against which his life with Joe at the forge must be measured.

CHAPTER 15

Summary

Pip has grown too old for the school of Mr. Wopsle's aunt, and Biddy has taught him everything she knows; thus he requests that Mr. Wopsle "bestow some intellectual crumbs upon |him|." He soon gives this up when he finds that all he listens to are Mr. Wopsle's tiring intellectual arguments. Whatever Pip learns, he tries to pass on to Joe for the following reason: "I wanted to make Joe less ignorant and common, that he might be worthier of my society and less open to Estella's approach." Though they go to the marshes for these lessons every Sunday afternoon, Joe's pleasure at the idea of increasing his knowledge does not disguise from Pip the fact that the blacksmith never remembers anything from one Sunday to another and, in truth, never learns anything at all. When Pip sees ships standing out at sea with their white sails, he thinks of Miss Havisham and Estella: they "and the strange house and the strange life appeared to have something to do with everything that was picturesque."

One afternoon Pip suggests to Joe that he visit Miss Havisham, to which the blacksmith responds negatively and suggests that she might assume that he wants or expects something. Pip acknowledges this but insists that he never properly thanked Miss Havisham for her kindness to him. Joe feels that if Pip does go, he should express his gratitude by taking a present made at the forge, though there is nothing made there that Miss Havisham does not already have. Pip points out that gratitude can probably best be expressed verbally, and unconsciously (though Joe does not perceive the significance of the slip) reveals that his actual motivation is a desire to see Estella. Joe agrees to the trip on the condition that it must be the last, unless Pip is encouraged to repeat his visit.

At the forge Joe keeps a journeyman helper named Orlick who pretends that his Christian name is Dolge; he is stubborn and a strong, dark-skinned fellow who always slouches and never appears in a hurry. He lives in the marshes and, convinced that Pip will replace him in his position at the forge, develops a strong dislike for the young apprentice. When Joe lets it be known that Pip is to have a half-holiday for his trip to Miss Havisham's, Orlick suggests that fairness demands his also receiving a half-holiday. Joe agrees, but when Mrs. Joe hears of this she goes into a rage, accusing Joe of wasting money by allowing the holiday. A bitter argument results in which Orlick calls Mrs. Joe "a foul shrew" and she becomes "blindly furious by regular stages," which leads Orlick to say that if he were her husband he would choke her. Mrs. Joe's fit leads Joe to challenge Orlick to a fight, and he knocks his employee unconscious. Later, when Pip comes down from dressing himself for his visit, he finds Joe and Orlick calmly drinking beer as if nothing had happened between them.

Arriving at Miss Havisham's, Pip is disappointed that the door is answered not by Estella but by Miss Sarah Pocket, who obviously regrets his being there and would send him away if she were willing to "hazard the responsibility." Initially Miss Havisham is cool, thinking that Pip wants something, but she warms when he assures her that he does not, and she further suggests that he visit her each year on his birthday. Seeing him look about, she displays "malignant enjoyment" and immediately tells him that Estella is abroad and being educated "for a lady." When Pip is dismissed, he goes to town and there meets Wopsle, who insists that he accompany him to Pumblechook's for a dramatic reading. The reading is both tedious and long; moreover, Pip finds himself the receiver of Wopsle's glares as the plot of the play (Lillo's *George Barnwell)* deals with the murder of an uncle by his nephew. At this moment the detested Pumblechook glares at his nephew Pip and says: "Take warning." With Wopsle, Pip begins to walk home through a heavy mist which feels wet and thick. A foreboding figure (which proves to be Orlick) rises from the mist and converses with them. Orlick comments that he has been in town and that cannons have fired to warn that again there has been an escape from the prison ships. They walk together and at the Three Jolly Bargemen see a great commotion. Investigating, Wopsle finds that the cause is a report of the Gargery's house having been entered and of there being an injury there. Pip rushes home, finding there Joe, a surgeon, and many other people. The cause is soon apparent: Mrs. Joe has been knocked down by a blow to her head and lies unconscious on the floor.

Commentary

This chapter achieves several purposes: it introduces the sinister figure of Orlick into the story and prepares us for his later villainy; it re-introduces the theme of crime and the part played by convicts in the novel; it also returns us to Satis House where we are caught up on the news of Estella's European education and prepared for future visits.

CHAPTER 16

Summary

The immediate memory of Wopsle's reading combines with Pip's guilty conscience, leading him to believe he had "some hand in the attack upon [his] sister" and that he is a prime suspect. However, the belief does not last, and evidence is soon uncovered to show that Mrs. Joe had been standing and facing the fire when she was attacked from behind, the assailant striking her on the head with a convict's filed leg-iron. Joe's examination of the weapon reveals that the filing had been done long ago (thus releasing the recently escaped convicts from suspicion), and Pip suspects that it is the iron filed from his convict's leg. He nevertheless does not suspect the convict himself; rather, he suspects "either Orlick, or the strange man who had shown [him] the file." Pip suspects Orlick because of the violent quarrel with Mrs. Joe. However, Orlick's account of being in town is confirmed. As to the man with the file, two facts suggest his innocence: the lack of motive (since Mrs. Joe was perfectly willing to return the money on request) and the absence of any evidence of a struggle before Mrs. Joe fell. Pip is conscience-stricken that he unintentionally supplied the weapon; yet (though for months he is tempted) he is unable to discuss the whole affair with Joe. The event of his meeting the convict is long past, and he fears that Joe will suspect him of lying and thus lose trust in him.

Mrs. Joe's movements, sight, hearing, and speech are damaged by the blow — though her temper is greatly improved and she appears far more patient. For some months there is difficulty in finding a suitable attendant, but finally (since Mr. Wopsle's great-aunt dies) Biddy becomes the housekeeper. Mrs. Joe's only method of communication is writing on a slate, and she draws numerous times an object which appears to be a hammer. Though Mrs. Joe's reasons for desiring such an object are obscure, they are finally figured out by Biddy. It is Orlick that Mrs. Joe wants to see; she has forgotten his name and can only associate him with the hammer. Though Pip expects her to denounce Orlick, he is surprised to note her "anxiety to be on good terms with him;" she shows every desire to pacify him and further displays in all that she does "an air of humble propitiation." After that event, a day scarcely passes that she does not draw the hammer and that Orlick does not slouch in and stand "doggedly before her, as if he knew no more than |Pip does| what to make of it."

Commentary

Dickens' interest in the law and in the nature of evidence has been widely noted. The reader should be aware that Pip's mind is not disciplined in legal matters (as most of his later conversations with Jaggers demonstrate); moreover, he is accepting as correct his initial opinion when Mrs. Joe's strange preference for Orlick is evidenced. The most significant piece of evidence (though Pip does not here recognize it) is that the weapon was a leg iron left in the marshes. As the reader already knows, Orlick lives in the marshes and must walk from his house to the forge each day.

CHAPTER 17

Summary

Pip's life now falls into a regular routine which is only interrupted by the arrival of his birthday and another visit to Miss Havisham's. She speaks of Estella in the same way and (when he is leaving) gives Pip a guinea and tells him to come again on his next birthday. The procedure is to be repeated annually and, since his initial reluctance to accepting the guinea is regarded as a sign of his expecting more, he decides to accept it on future visits. The changeless quality of Miss Havisham and her home while all outside grows older bewilders Pip and influences him to hate his trade even more and to become more ashamed of his home. In the meantime, Biddy (though she is common, not beautiful, and could not be like Estella) grows neater, brighter, and more attractive: "she had curiously thoughtful and attentive eyes; eyes that were very pretty and very good." However, Pip's vanity about his growing knowledge is somewhat deflated by the fact that Biddy seems to know everything that he knows. He admires her taking advantage of every opportunity; yet his unconsciously condescending tone brings tears to her eyes and he comes to realize that he has never really expressed his gratitude for her having been his first teacher. This realization and his own unhappiness lead him to take Biddy into his confidence. On Sunday afternoon they walk together in the marshes and Pip is again affected by the sails of ships which recall to him Estella and Miss Havisham. He tells Biddy that he wants to be a gentleman and that he is miserable with his work and with his life; her opinion is that he would be less happy as a gentleman. He regrets the fact that he cannot enjoy his work, be happy in his home and social surroundings, and perhaps someday marry Biddy. Instead of this, he adds, he has been called "coarse and common" by a girl to whom he is greatly attracted. Biddy then asks an important question: "Do you want to be a gentleman, to spite her or to gain her over?" Pip does not know the answer, and Biddy (reasonable as ever) suggests that either alternative could be better confronted by a course of action other than his present one: "That |i.e., to spite her| might be better and more independently done by caring nothing for words. And if it is to gain her over, I should think — but you know best — she was not worth gaining." Pip admits the truth of this but says he cannot help himself. "Vaguely convinced that |he| was very much ill-used by somebody, or by everybody," Pip cries a bit; and Biddy stops trying to reason and starts comforting him. She thanks him for his confidence and then answers his promise that he shall always so confide in her: "Till you're a gentleman." Biddy's humanity and rightness overwhelm Pip when he thinks of her in comparison to Estella; aloud he voices the wish that he could fall in love with her. She answers meekly: "But you never will, you see." Approaching the churchyard, the couple is suddenly interrupted by the appearance of Orlick, who rises "from the gate, or from the rushes, or from the ooze (which was quite in his stagnant way)." Orlick wants to accompany them, but Pip objects; then Orlick laughs but follows them at a distance. Biddy tells Pip she dislikes Orlick because he seems to like her, a comment which startles Pip and leads him to stay between Orlick and Biddy as much as possible. Then Pip falls into confusion; he thinks of Estella and Miss Havisham, then of Joe and Biddy. In his mind he compares the different lives and social positions which they represent.

Commentary

Though externally the comparison in this chapter appears to be between the world represented by Satis House and that represented by the simple virtues of Joe and Biddy, the reader is more aware of a contrast between Pip's powers of perception and those of Biddy. He aspires to greatness, she accepts what she has; and part of her acceptance is a recognition that Pip's aspirations amount to a permanent state. She knows his confidence in her is but a whim of the moment just as she is sure he can never love her — though Pip himself is not so sure. Moreover, she accepts condescension from him which he is only momentarily aware of displaying. She is a realist who can see; he is a romanticist who is blind, and his blindness is evidenced most notably by his never perceiving the fact that Biddy loves him.

CHAPTER 18

Summary

On a Saturday night, in the fourth year of Pip's apprenticeship, he and Joe sit at the Three Jolly Bargemen listening to Mr. Wopsle's account of a recently committed murder. In the background is a strange gentleman who displays contempt and bites "the side of a great forefinger as he [watches] the group of faces;" suddenly the man interrupts, demonstrating the false logic of Wopsle's arbitrary judgment that the suspect charged with the murder is guilty. Displaying a thorough knowledge of English law, he clearly shows Wopsle to be a fool. Turning from his triumph, the stranger (whom Pip immediately recognizes as the gentleman he had met on the stairs on the occasion of his second visit to Miss Havisham's) asks aloud for Joe Gargery and for his apprentice Pip. He has a message to convey and suggests that it be given privately at Joe's cottage. On arriving there, the man introduces himself as a London lawyer named Jaggers; he is a "confidential agent of another" and is carrying out a duty which, if his own opinion had been asked, would have resulted in his not being there at all. The duty entails his being the bearer of an offer to relieve Joe of his apprentice Pip, and he is authorized to request that Joe cancel Pip's papers (either freely or by payment of a fee). Joe, who would never stand in Pip's way, says he will freely release Pip and will not accept money for doing so, a choice which Jaggers obviously feels is a foolish one. The lawyer continues, now referring to Pip: "The communication I have got to make is, that he has Great Expectations." Both Joe and Pip gasp, but they listen further as the lawyer says Pip is to come into "a handsome property" and that the donor's desire is "that he be immediately removed from his present sphere of life and from this place, and be brought up as a gentleman — in a word, as a young fellow of great expectations."

Pip immediately assumes that "sober reality" has replaced his dreams and wild fancy: Miss Havisham has made his "fortune on a grand scale." Two conditions are stated by the lawyer: first, Pip must always bear the name of Pip, and, second, the name of the benefactor is to remain a secret which is never to be discussed and will only be revealed when the donor so chooses (perhaps years later). Pip accepts, and Jaggers immediately makes it known that he is to be the boy's guardian, to deliver money (which he holds in trust) at appointed intervals, and to provide for his education. Pip recognizes the name of Matthew Pocket, whom Jaggers mentions as a possible tutor for him; he accepts the suggestion, and Jaggers gives him money to secure a proper wardrobe before going to London (which Pip says he will do immediately). Then Jaggers turns to the dumbfounded Joe, asking if he is sure he does not require compensation for the loss of his apprentice. At this Joe breaks down, referring painfully to the young Pip and the life he had thought to share with him, and says, while he certainly will not stand in Pip's way, that money can be no compensation for the loss. Pip is emotionally touched by the scene, especially when Jaggers' continued offers lead Joe to jump up and threaten the lawyer with a fight if he does not stop baiting him. Pip calms Joe and (after Jaggers has again said he has no opinion about the whole affair and that he is merely being paid for his services) asks Jaggers suggestively whether there would be any objection to his saying goodbye to certain friends (meaning Miss Havisham, whom he thinks to be his benefactress). Jaggers agrees and leaves.

Joe and Pip stare silently into the fire, neither able to speak. Finally Pip asks if Joe has told Biddy, which he has not, and requests that he do so. Joe blurts it out simply: "Pip's a gentleman of fortun', then, and God bless him in it!" Then both Biddy and Joe heartily congratulate him, a response which he slightly resents because there is "a certain touch of sadness in their congratulation" and because their wonder seems to be so great that *he* could be a gentleman. Biddy tries to explain the event to Mrs. Joe, but the poor woman's mind is so damaged that she cannot understand. Joe and Biddy become more cheerful, and Pip (the narrator relating the story many years later) concludes that his initial dissatisfaction at their response may have been, without his quite knowing it, dissatisfaction with himself.

To avoid being stared at and feeling coarse at the forge, Pip decides to have his new clothes sent to Pumblechook's, though he dreads the idea of being observed by Wopsle and the Hubbles. Biddy ironically asks Pip when he will show them how he looks in his fine new clothes, a question which Pip resents because of the suggestion that he would do otherwise. Pip says goodnight and thinks joyfully of soon rising above the humble cottage; yet within him there still exists a dilemma which points out the opposition between "the forge and Miss Havisham's, and Biddy and Estella." He sees a lonely Joe standing below and smoking his pipe, sees him joined by Biddy, and hears them speak of him in endearing tones. He feels "it very sorrowful and strange that this first night of |his| bright fortunes should be the loneliest |he| had ever known." In his bed he never again "slept the old sound sleep."

Commentary

Dickens here clearly stresses the fact that, while Pip appears to be receiving a great blessing, the young apprentice's losses actually overshadow his gains. Jaggers considers Joe a "village idiot" because he accepts no money in exchange for his apprentice; the basis of this judgment, the substitution of money for feelings and for people, characterizes the social circle into which Pip is soon to move. For Joe no amount of money can compensate for his loss; for Pip, a few moments have so changed his life that he even resents a display of feeling on the part of Joe and Biddy and will willingly sacrifice them for the "great expectations" made possible by unexpected money. Pip's second and greatest sacrifice is that of a stable social circle; he can never again sleep "the old sound sleep" because he was born an orphan who — through luck — came to be an apprentice to one who loved him. He was not born a gentleman and, instead of self-confident acceptance, the social climber must always accept a defensive position, a position which characteristically and naturally brings sleepless nights with it. Already Pip's acceptance of this defensive position is obvious: he resents Joe's and Biddy's wonder that *he* should be a gentleman; he resents what he thinks to be their mistrust; he is embarrassed at the potential response to his new dress; and he is conscience-stricken by his own coldness as compared with the feeling obvious in the "endearing tones" of Biddy and Joe. Most of all, he is concerned by the fact that his defense is vulnerable: Biddy knows him for what he has become — a snob.

CHAPTER 19

Summary

Pip awakens cheerfully and only regrets that there are still six days between the present and the time of his departure for London. Together he and Joe burn his papers, and he feels a sense of freedom. Experiencing the novelty of his liberation, he goes to church with Joe and refuses to take seriously the theme of the sermon which concerns the difficulty of a rich man's entering the Kingdom of Heaven. Looking at the congregation, he feels "a sublime compassion for the poor creatures" who are destined to attend a service there every Sunday of their lives and resolves that someday he will "do something for them," perhaps give everyone a great feast "and a gallon of condescension." He thinks with shame of his association with the convict but takes some pleasure in the fact that "it happened a long time ago, and that he had doubtless been transported a long way off, and that he was dead to |him|, and might be veritably dead into the bargain." Happily thinking of London, his expectations, and Miss Havisham's apparent intentions for him and Estella, Pip goes to sleep on the marsh. When he awakes Joe is sitting beside him and reveals that he has concluded that Pip will never forget their friendship. The former apprentice is not pleased with "Joe's being so mightily secure" of a gentleman, but he says nothing. Nevertheless, he does regret the fact that Joe is not better educated — though Joe fails to understand Pip's subtlety in implying that it would then be easier for a gentleman to help a blacksmith. Later, Pip suggests that Biddy devote herself to improving Joe's education and his manners so as to increase the ease with which Pip can raise Joe's status. Quietly and ironically, Biddy displays a fury at his arrogance. She questions whether Pip supposes Joe may too have pride, a question to which Pip responds with contempt and thus leads her to add: "Pride is not all of one kind." Angered by her remark, Pip demands that she continue, and she does: "He [Joe] may be too proud to let anyone take him out of a place that he is competent to fill, and fills well and with respect." With "a virtuous and superior tone," Pip neglects her comment and attributes it to envy, a remark which obviously both hurts her and leads her to assert that whatever opinion he takes away of her will not alter her opinion of him — "yet a gentleman should not be unjust neither."

Sleeping is as difficult on the second night of Pip's fortune as on the first, but morning again brightens his views and he goes to see Mr. Trabb, the tailor. Trabb greets him pleasantly; yet his tone changes, and becomes more respectful, when Pip lets his good luck be known and states his desire to buy "a fashionable suit of clothes." Trabb's boy, however, greets Pip by sweeping over his shoes and later knocks his broom about as if to express "equality with any blacksmith, alive or dead." Trabb sternly scolds the boy, and after Pip has made all his purchases he remarks that his first "decided experience of the stupendous power of money" is seeing Trabb's boy put in his place. Immediately he goes to Pumblechook, who flatters Pip in a way that he has come to think his new position deserves. He feeds Pip, lets it be known that he also thinks Miss Havisham to be the source of the good fortune, frequently shakes his hand, and uses the expression "May I" so many times that it becomes a refrain. Pip so enjoys Pumblechook's humbleness that he concludes his earlier opinion of his uncle has been a false one; he now assumes him to be "a sensible practical good-hearted prime fellow." Pumblechook's last act is to offer Pip a partnership in the seed business in exchange for capital, a proposal which Pip decides to reject for the time. Then he leaves, followed by his uncle who desires one last handshake.

On Friday (three days later), Pip goes to his uncle's and puts on his "eagerly expected garments." Their elegance falls below his expectation, but he decides to wear them for his interview with Miss Havisham. Pip's appearance shocks Sarah Pocket, who answers the door, but Miss Havisham says she has heard of his good fortune from Jaggers and waves her crutch around Pip "as if she, the fairy godmother, who had changed [him] were bestowing the finishing gift." She lets it be known that she knows all the details of the arrangement with Jaggers, then triumphantly allows Pip — still in the presence of the envious Sarah — to kneel, kiss her hand, and say goodbye. He returns to Pumblechook's, takes off his fine clothes, and carries them in a bundle back to Joe's cottage. Tomorrow is the day for Pip's departure, and as the time passes he becomes "more and more appreciative of the society of Joe and Biddy." They have a fine evening meal together, though all are in very low spirits. Pip requests that he walk alone to the coach the next morning, for (he believes privately) there would be too great a contrast between himself and Joe. Awaking the next morning to the smell of Biddy's cooking, Pip rises and eats a hurried breakfast before departing. The last thing he sees is Joe and Biddy tearfully throwing old shoes after him. At the edge of the village Pip cries, becoming "more sorry, more aware of |his| own ingratitude, more gentle." Getting on the coach, he considers going back for a better parting, but by the time he resolves his dilemma the coach is too far gone: "And the mists had all solemnly risen now, and the world lay spread before me." This ends the first stage of Pip's expectations.

SUMMARY OF IMPORTANT DEVELOPMENTS

1. The convict theme, which reappears, is introduced.
2. Pip's ambitions are aroused by visiting Satis House and meeting Estella.
3. Miss Havisham's interest in Pip leads him to expect that she has some special purpose in mind for him.
4. We have heard of Matthew Pocket and his son, who are to play a significant role in Pip's development in Stage II.
5. Mrs. Joe, the terror of Pip's young life, has been mysteriously attacked and is rendered an invalid.
6. Orlick is presented as an evil figure in the background.
7. Biddy is becoming more attractive and more prominent in Pip's life.
8. There is a struggle in Pip's mind between his ambition and his sense of duty to his loyal friends.
9. Mr. Jaggers announces that Pip's hopes of advancement are to be fulfilled by an unknown benefactor.
10. On the lap of good fortune, and in a world whose attitude to him is now one of respect, Pip departs for London, still not completely happy, yet certain that he will find happiness.

Stage II of Pip's Great Expectations
CHAPTER 20

Summary
The journey to London takes about five hours, and Pip arrives just after noon. The size of the city frightens him, and he is surprised to note that it is "rather ugly, crooked, narrow, and dirty." The coachman who takes Pip to Jaggers' office voices fear at any prospect of getting in trouble with Jaggers. In the front office Pip is told that Jaggers is in court and that he should wait for him in the inner chamber. The chamber is "a most dismal place," lit only by skylight.

Pip notices an old rusty pistol, a sword in a scabbard, several strange boxes and packages, two dreadful casts of distorted faces, and Jaggers' own highbacked chair (which looks like a coffin). The wait in those dismal surroundings makes Pip nervous, and he decides to go for a brief walk in the surrounding area. The area, however, is even more dirty and depressing, and a drunken jailor shows him the gallows at Newgate Prison. Pip notes that people around him are also awaiting Jaggers, and the lawyer's approach leads the mob to move toward him. Jaggers takes Pip by his side and interviews other clients as they walk along. All of Jaggers' clients appear to be both desperate and members of a lower (and sometimes criminal) class. After concluding his business, Jaggers tells Pip that plans are made for him to stay at Barnard's Inn with young Herbert Pocket. On Monday the two will go to Matthew Pocket's where Pip may begin his studies. Finally the lawyer gives Pip a liberal allowance of money, tells him that his credit is good, and says he will try to keep him out of financial trouble. To this he adds: "Of course you'll go wrong somehow, but that's no fault of mine." Pip leaves, accompanied by Wemmick (Jaggers' clerk) who is to lead him to Barnard's Inn.

Commentary

This chapter marks the beginning of Pip's life as a London gentleman. The appearance of London proves disappointing to Pip, and this is only the first and very minor instance of reality not fulfilling the expectations of Pip's active imagination.

This chapter also introduces us to Wemmick, Mr. Jaggers' clerk, an unusual individual in many ways. It is Wemmick who looks after the financial aspect of Pip's career, but he plays an even more important role as Pip's confidant later on in the novel.

CHAPTER 21

Summary

Wemmick is a middle-aged "dry man, rather short in stature, with a square wooden face, whose expression seemed to have been imperfectly chipped out with a dull-edged chisel." His frayed shirt indicates that he is a bachelor, and his numerous mourning rings and other such articles suggest that he has suffered "a good many bereavements." Wemmick tells Pip that London, like anywhere else, is a good place in which to be cheated, robbed, and murdered; criminals multiply here not because of bad blood, but simply because "they'll do it, if there's anything to be got by it." Pip notes too that the clerk walks "in a self-contained way as if there were nothing in the streets to claim his attention. His mouth was such a post-office of a mouth that he had a mechanical appearance of smiling." When Pip asks Wemmick if he knows Matthew Pocket, he is slightly depressed that the clerk's affirmative reply is accompanied by "an air of toleration or depreciation." This depression increases as Pip views Barnard's Inn; it is a run-down and partially occupied decaying structure which appears so covered by smoke and ash as to be "undergoing penance and humiliation as a mere dust-hole." Wemmick tells Pip that he keeps the cash and thus they shall meet often; then he leaves him at the proper place to await the return of young Herbert Pocket. About a half hour later, a boy Pip's own age appears on the stairway. Pip stares as if in a dream while the boy talks; then a mutual recognition takes place. Herbert Pocket is the pale young gentleman with whom Pip had fought at Satis House.

Commentary

The new link with Miss Havisham (Matthew and Herbert Pocket are her relatives) confirms Pip's suspicions that Miss Havisham is his benefactress.

Notice Dickens' use of coincidence. Dickens frequently introduces a character early in the novel and leaves his identity or importance unrevealed until a later time. Although Pip does not yet realize it, it is coincidence, and not the design of Miss Havisham, that has him meet up with both Herbert and Jaggers again after his brief encounters with them long ago at Satis House.

CHAPTER 22

Summary

Pip and Herbert stand staring at one another; then both burst out laughing. When Herbert apologizes for having beaten him, Pip concludes that the boy has "confounded his intention with the execution," but he does not contradict him and replies modestly, after which they shake hands warmly. Herbert recalls that on that earlier day Miss Havisham had invited him "to see if she could take a fancy to [him], but she did not and he is just as happy with the result" (for now he is not engaged to Estella). He tells Pip that Estella was an orphan. He also comments: "That girl's hard and haughty and capricious to the last degree, and has been brought up by Miss Havisham to wreak vengeance on all the male sex." Pip is quite interested in all of this, and Herbert promises to relate the rest of the tale at dinner. Pip informs Herbert that Jaggers is his guardian; Herbert explains that Jaggers is also Miss Havisham's lawyer and that Matthew Pocket (his father) was known to Jaggers through the Havisham connection. Matthew is Miss Havisham's cousin, but he is out of her favor because "he is a bad courtier and will not propitiate her." Pip immediately recognizes the means of his being brought together with Herbert; he further admires the "frank and easy way" of his new acquaintance and sees in him "a natural incapacity to do anything secret and mean." Of Herbert's future Pip thinks: "There was something wonderfully hopeful about his genial air, and something that at the same time whispered to me he would never be very successful or rich."

Because Herbert is so talkative, Pip decides to drop his own reserve and relate his story; he explains that the life he has led has not been geared to developing the manners of a gentleman, and requests that Herbert aid him by giving hints "whenever he saw |him| at a loss or going wrong." Pip agrees to Herbert's calling him Handel, a name made appropriate by "a charming piece of music by Handel, called the Harmonious Blacksmith." He enjoys the independence of eating dinner with no older people around and soon reminds Herbert of his promise to continue on the subject of Miss Havisham. Herbert's story is as follows: Miss Havisham was a spoiled child whose mother died when she was a baby and whose father (a country gentleman and brewer) denied her nothing. Both Mr. Havisham and his daughter were "very rich and very proud." Mr. Havisham privately married his cook, by whom he had a son, and he did not tell his daughter what he had done until the death of his second wife. Then the son was taken into the house; "he turned out riotous, extravagant, undutiful — altogether bad." Finally his father disinherited him, but softened and left him money — though not nearly so much as he left his daughter. As an heiress, Miss Havisham was much courted and looked upon as a great match. The half-brother immediately ran into debt, and (so it is suspected) "cherished a deep and mortal grudge against her as having influenced the father's anger." Then a man appeared who pursued her; he was not a gentleman (though his external appearance suggested that he was) and, after she had begun to idolize him, he used her love to get great sums of money from her. Also, he led her to buy her brother's share of the brewery at an immense price "on the plea that when he was her husband he must hold and manage it all." She had no objective advice, since all her relatives except Matthew were poor, scheming and jealous. The result was that when Matthew warned her against putting herself in the man's power, she accused him in the presence of her intended husband of "being disappointed in the hope of fawning upon her for his own advancement" and ordered him out of the house (to which he never returned). A day for the marriage was fixed and all preparations made; then, at twenty minutes to nine on the wedding day, a letter arrived as Miss Havisham was dressing for her marriage. It heartlessly broke off the wedding, the result being: "When she recovered from a bad illness that she had, she laid the whole place waste, . . . and she has never since looked upon the light of day." It has been supposed that her fiancé and the half-brother "acted throughout in concert . . . that it was a conspiracy between them; and that they shared the profits." At last the two men, even after carrying out their scheme, fell "into deeper shame and degradation" — financial ruin.

This is all Herbert knows, and he immediately assures Pip that he will never raise the subject of the source of his good fortune (thus leading Pip to assume he "perfectly understood Miss Havisham to be [his] benefactress"). Herbert likewise lets it be known that he considers his own present position in a counting house as a mere step on his way to financial success as an insurer of ships. Living in a private dream world, he bears the poverty of his present position with the same kind of cheerfulness he accepted his physical defeat at Satis House. Pip and Herbert enjoy each other's company; they go for walks, attend the theater, go to church, and visit the parks. On Monday afternoon they go to Matthew Pocket's house in Hammersmith. Entering the garden, Pip notes the many children and is greeted by Mrs. Pocket. She hardly notices the disturbance caused by the children and serenely leaves their care to Flopson and Millers, two nurses. When Matthew finally appears, Pip is not surprised to find that he is "a gentleman with a rather perplexed expression of face, and with his very grey hair disordered on his head, as if he didn't quite see his way to putting anything straight."

CHAPTER 23

Summary

Matthew Pocket greets Pip warmly. He is young looking, appears unaffected and prevents his absent-minded way from appearing ridiculous by the fact that he is aware it is very near being so. Mrs. Pocket is the only daughter of an unclear line of nobility; she was "brought up from her cradle as one who in the nature of things must marry a title, and who was to be guarded from the acquisition of plebeian domestic knowledge." The result is that she is "highly ornamental, but perfectly helpless and useless," while at the same time she is pitied because she had not married a title. Mr. Pocket takes Pip to a pleasant room, then introduces him to two other students: Bentley Drummle, "an old-looking young man of a heavy order of architecture" who is heir to a title, and Startop, younger in appearance and apparently more studious. From Herbert Pip learns that Matthew had distinguished himself at Harrow and Cambridge; then, after marrying Mrs. Pocket, his prospects had been dimmed and he had taken up a position as tutor. After tiring of this, he had gone to London where he gradually failed in "loftier hopes." Now, unable to support the aristocratic habits of his wife, he has returned to a position as tutor in order to maintain the house. At dinner, Mrs. Pocket, Mrs. Coiler ("a toady neighbour"), and Drummle discuss aristocracy and nobility, the only subject which interests Mrs. Pocket. A servant brings news that the beef is misplaced, and an excited Matthew amazes Pip by attempting to lift himself from his chair by pulling his own hair. The dreamy

Mrs. Pocket hardly notices her children when they enter, and she continues her conversation with Drummle. Mr. and Mrs. Pocket twice have brief domestic quarrels, and in the evening Pip goes rowing on the river with Drummle and Startop.

Commentary
The entertaining account of Mrs. Pocket's snobbery is a variation in caricature on the theme of Pip's snobbery. Although both Mrs. Pocket and Bentley Drummle see themselves as aristocratic types, neither of them has a very valid claim to that distinction; Mrs. Pocket is without money and Drummle has nothing but money to recommend him. Pip's almost immediate disliking for Drummle is significant in view of Drummle's later involvement with Estella.

CHAPTER 24

Summary
After two or three days, Mr. Pocket and Pip have a long talk; Pip then finds that his education is not to be designed for any profession, but merely to make him able to "hold his own" with the average man in prosperous circumstances.

From Wemmick Pip learns that Jaggers' obscure, logical, and gruff manner is a professional pose; he could not succeed with his types of clients unless he had it. Wemmick's motto is based on the same cautious considerations which underlie Jaggers' manner; it is simply "Get hold of portable property." Wemmick invites Pip to visit his home; he further suggests that an invitation for dinner from Jaggers is forthcoming. On the latter occasion, Wemmick suggests, Pip should note Jaggers' housekeeper, "A wild beast tamed" by the lawyer's powers. Finally, Wemmick and Pip go to see Jaggers in court, and Pip immediately notes that his guardian is master of the situation: Jaggers has "taken down" any testimony with which he does not agree; he threatens and terrifies witnesses; the magistrates shiver "under a single bite of his finger;" and "thieves and thieftakers hung in dread rapture on his words." Pip cannot determine which side the lawyer argues, "for he seemed . . . to be grinding the whole place in a mill."

Commentary
The need for a pose or a façade is here finally established for Pip. Even in the most difficult circumstances, Jaggers' manner both protects and gives him the upper hand. Wemmick's motto, the need for acquiring "portable property," is also a professional pose, but Pip does not yet have any way of knowing this. By coming to see wealth and disguise as mutually interrelated, admirable attributes, Pip is growing farther and farther from the humble ethical system represented by Joe and

Biddy. Moreover, he does not yet realize that desire for property and disguise can lead, when employed by a person of lesser abilities than Jaggers, to no more than the life represented by Pumblechook.

CHAPTER 25

Summary

Drummle is sulky, arrogant, idle, reserved, and suspicious; he comes from a rich family in Somersetshire who endured his characteristics until they discovered that he was "a blockhead." Startop had been spoiled by his mother and kept at home rather than being sent to school; yet he is devoted to his mother, and Pip finds him much more agreeable than Drummle. When the three go rowing, Drummle is indifferent to the others' company and rows behind in their wake. Miss Havisham's relatives (Georgianna, Camilla, and her husband) visit Matthew, and they flatter Pip though they actually resent his good fortune. During this period, Pip is an industrious student, though within a few months he acquires quite expensive habits. Since he has not seen Wemmick for some weeks, he writes a note and proposes going home with him one evening. Wemmick is pleased, and when they meet at Jaggers' office he tells Pip that his guardian plans to entertain both him and his three friends (Herbert, Drummle, and Startop). He further explains that Jaggers never fastens a door or window at night; no thief would dare steal from him.

Pip and Wemmick arrive at Wemmick's home in the district of Walworth; it is "a little wooden cottage in the midst of plots of garden, and the top of it was cut out and painted like a battery mounted with guns." It has fake gothic windows and a gothic door almost too small to get in; there is also a flagstaff on which Wemmick runs up a flag on Sundays, a small plank which acts as a drawbridge over a "chasm" about four feet wide and two deep, and a gun which is fired each night at nine o'clock. Behind the "castle" are a pig, fowls, rabbits, and a garden, all of which provide food — if necessary — with no help from the outside world. Wemmick acknowledges Pip's compliments and introduces him to the Aged, his father who is "sitting by a fire, a very old man in a flannel coat: clean, cheerful, comfortable, and well cared for, but intensely deaf." Though the Aged cannot hear, he enjoys receiving nods; thus both Pip and Wemmick nod numerous times. Wemmick explains that it took years to perfect his castle, and when Pip expresses wonder about Jaggers' response to this, Wemmick answers that his employer has never seen it. He explains to Pip:

> The office is one thing, and private life is another. When I go into the office, I leave the Castle behind me, and when I come into the Castle, I leave the office behind me. If it's not in any

way disagreeable to you, you'll oblige me by doing the same. I don't wish it professionally spoken about.

At nine o'clock the gun is fired from the Battery (much to the Aged's enjoyment) and Wemmick shows Pip his "collection of curiosities." Pip has an excellent dinner and night's rest. The next morning after breakfast he and Wemmick leave for Jaggers' office. "By degrees, Wemmick got dryer and harder as [they] went along, and his mouth tightened into a post office again." At last, when they arrive at Jaggers' office, Wemmick's appearance leads Pip to decide that the spectacle at Walworth has been completely pushed from Wemmick's mind.

Commentary
Wemmick's function is obviously twofold: first, he represents a course of action which Pip might himself adopt as a way of maintaining integrity in relation to the two worlds which he inhabits (that of the gentleman and that of the forge); and, second, he clarifies (by the very fact that Pip cannot understand his two-sided character) the very single-mindedness toward which Pip has directed himself. Unlike Wemmick and (partially) Jaggers, Pip's facade has become his reality. The world of Joe and Biddy no longer exists for him; he can never experience in relation to Joe the kind of pleasure experienced by Wemmick in his service and kindness to the Aged. Wemmick willingly makes of himself a "split personality;" Pip willingly suppresses any feelings which would lead him to fulfil obligations to those who inhabited his former society. The irony is that Pip finds Wemmick's hardness, his devotion to "portable property," less admirable than his rural virtues; he does not perceive that this aspect of Wemmick serves as a mirror for his own devotion to the power of money.

CHAPTER 26

Summary
When Pip enters Jaggers' office after the trip from Walworth, his guardian extends the invitation to him and his friends which Wemmick had suggested was forthcoming. Pip notes that after each interview with clients, Jaggers washes his hands — thus washing "his clients off, as if he were a surgeon or a dentist." He has a room fitted for the purpose; it smells "of the scented soap like a perfumer's shop." Pip and his friends are to meet Jaggers at his office, from which they will go together to his home. When they arrive at six o'clock, Jaggers seems to have been working on a darker case than usual: he not only washes his hands, but washes his face, gargles, and scrapes his nails with a penknife. They go to Jaggers' house, which Pip finds "rather a stately house of its kind, but dolefully in want of painting, and with dirty win-

dows;" the hall is "bare, gloomy, and little used." The dinner is "comfortably laid" but not elegant. Throughout the meal, Jaggers keeps everything under his own hand and distributes everything himself. To Pip's surprise, Jaggers seemed "at once to be principally, if not solely, interested in Drummle," whom he calls the Spider and with whom he begins to converse. Of Drummle he says: "I like the look of that fellow." The housekeeper enters to serve dinner: she appears to be about forty and is "rather tall, of a lithe nimble figure, extremely pale, with large faded eyes, and a quantity of streaming hair." To Pip she seems both curious and wild; he also recognizes that her every act is preceded by a look at Jaggers which seems to suggest the awaiting of instructions.

Dinner goes off gaily; yet Pip perceives that Jaggers "wrenched the weakest part of our dispositions out of us." Pip himself comes to confess his tendency toward extravagant spending, to patronize Herbert, and to boast of his prospects. Drummle brags of his superiority as a rower, and soon all (unconsciously through Jaggers' prodding) resort "to baring and spanning |their| arms in a ridiculous manner." Suddenly Jaggers stops the foolish contest; he tells them that if they talk of strength, they must see Molly's (the housekeeper's) wrist. Her hands are large and strong; one wrist is "much disfigured — deeply scarred and scarred across and across." As the hands are shown, Molly looks at each of the boys; then she is dismissed. Jaggers drinks a toast to Drummle; then he views him with interest, the boy displaying "a sulky triumph" and a "morose depreciation of the rest . . . until he became downright intolerable." All talk too much, and Pip and Drummle begin an argument about lending money. Jaggers stops the disagreement by announcing it is half past nine and that the evening is concluded. They all leave; then Pip returns to apologize for the disagreement that took place. When Pip admits his dislike of Drummle, Jaggers says: "Keep as clear of him as you can. But I like the fellow, Pip; he is one of the true sort." A month later, Drummle's studies are completed, to the relief of all but Mrs. Pocket. Drummle leaves for home.

CHAPTER 27

Summary

Pip receives an apologetic letter from Biddy; she writes at the request of Joe, informing Pip that he is coming to London next day with Wopsle and wishes to see him. She adds that Mrs. Joe is the same, that he (Pip) is the subject of many of their conversations, and in a postscript says that Joe wishes her to add to the letter "what larks." Pip would pay money to keep the visit from taking place, but his dread is lessened by the fact that Joe's country ways will only be seen by Herbert, whom he respects, and not by Drummle, whom he despises.

("So, throughout life, our worst weaknesses and meannesses are usually committed for the sake of the people whom we most despise.") Recently Pip has expensively re-decorated his apartment at Barnard's Inn and has also acquired a servant in uniform for whom he has "to find . . . a little to do and a great deal to eat." As the time for Joe's visit approaches, Pip would like to run away. Instead he places his servant (called "the Avenger") on duty in the hall and awaits Joe, whom he soon recognizes "by his clumsy manner of coming upstairs."

The servant announces Joe, who wipes his feet before entering and then approaches with "his good honest face all glowing and shining." The scene so impresses the blacksmith that he does not know what to do with his hat; he soon becomes more relaxed and tells his little news, including the fact that Wopsle is in London because "he's left the Church and went into the playacting." Herbert enters, thus adding to Joe's confusion, and the situation becomes intolerable when Pip objects to Joe's calling him "Sir." Finally, Herbert leaves for work and Joe (seemingly conscious that Pip is disgusted with his behavior) comes to the point of his visit. His message is that he had been summoned by Miss Havisham, who sends word to Pip that "Estella has come home, and would be glad to see him." Pip blushes, aware that had he known Joe's errand, he would have given him more encouragement. Concluding his duty, Joe wishes Pip well and prepares to leave. When Pip protests his leaving, Joe answers that sometimes divisions come and must be met; he adds that the two should only be seen together in private and not in London, where Joe's clothes (obviously uncomfortable to him) do not meet the social standard. In a heart-rending sentence, he tells Pip to see him at the forge: "You won't find half so much fault in me if you think of me in my forge dress, with my hammer in my hand, or even my pipe." Pip is touched by the comments and recognizes "a simple dignity in him." After his old friend leaves, he follows him into the street — but Joe has gone.

Commentary

The result of Pip's respect for money is made all too evident when contrasted with the humble virtues of Joe and Biddy. Only with the mention of Estella, the figure who potentially represents the next rung in Pip's intended ladder to success, is Pip's attention drawn to his friend for any other purpose than to find fault with his appearance and actions. In Pip's pose, Joe does not see the boy he knew — only the figure of a gentleman to whom he can refer as "Sir." Pip recognizes the gap, but criticizes Joe for using an expression which signifies that the recognition is mutual. Pip knows that for Joe to feel the need to call him "Sir" signifies that he is both an ingrate and, more notably, a snob. He is not willing to acknowledge that Joe has penetrated his façade and is correct in the judgment.

CHAPTER 28

Summary

Pip sees clearly that he must go to the country next day, and in initial repentance for his treatment of Joe, he decides to stay at the blacksmith's cottage. He soon willingly fools himself, however, and decides to stay at the Blue Boar, an inn. Pip hesitates but decides to go on the same coach which carries two convicts in irons. To his surprise, he recognizes one of them as the man with the file who had long ago given him money at the Three Jolly Bargemen. Though Pip sits directly in front of him, he is not recognized, even when the convict discusses the incident with his companion. From their conversation, Pip learns that the gift was not a mistake: the convict had been a messenger commissioned by the convict for whom Pip had stolen food and a file. The coincidence of their being together in the coach leads Pip to dread that he may be recognized; thus as he leaves the coach his fancy conjures up a vision of "the boat with its convict crew waiting for them at the slime-washed stairs." Walking from the coach to the Blue Boar, his fear is "altogether undefined and vague," but it is great fear nevertheless. At the Blue Boar he is recognized by a waiter who gives him a dirty old copy of the local newspaper; it carries a feature story which suggests that Pip's fortune is due to the efforts of Pumblechook.

CHAPTER 29

Summary

Pip rises next morning too early to go to Miss Havisham's. He loiters about, deciding to go to Joe's next day and thinking of Miss Havisham's supposed adoption of both Estella and himself and of her seeming intention to bring them together in marriage. He imagines a romance in which he is the young knight and hero, and Estella is the princess. However, through this romantic veil Pip sees the truth: he loves Estella simply because he finds her irresistible. Often, if not always, he loves her "against reason, against promise, against peace, against hope, against happiness, against all discouragement that could be." He loves her in spite of — or because of — these facts. Arriving at Miss Havisham's gate, he is surprised to be met by Orlick, who has become her porter during Pip's absence. Pip enters and, as he passes through a corridor, meets the envious Sarah Pocket, "who appeared to have now become constitutionally green and yellow by reason of |him|" and whose only comment is that she hopes Matthew Pocket's family is wiser. All is the same with Miss Havisham and her surroundings, though Pip notes sitting near her "an elegant lady whom [he] had never seen." Soon it dawns on him that the lady is Estella, so much more beautiful and feminine that his own change seems nothing to him.

In his mind, her appearance makes him slip "hopelessly back into the coarse and common boy again." "With her greedy look," Miss Havisham asks if he finds Estella changed. During his confused conversation, he notes that Estella still treats him as a boy, but lures him on. Estella's wilful qualities and her pride are now a part of her beauty. Likewise, it is

> . . . impossible to dissociate her presence from all those wretched hankerings after money and gentility that have disturbed [his] boyhood . . . In a word, it was impossible for [him] to separate her, in the past or in the present, from the innermost life of [his] life.

It is decided that Pip should spend the rest of the day at Satis House, and Miss Havisham sends him and Estella to walk in the neglected garden. They talk of Pip's new life, of the day long ago when she secretly watched the fight with Herbert, and of her making Pip cry. Estella's not even remembering the last of these leads him to cry inwardly again. Then she warns him that she has no heart, no softness, no sympathy, no sentiment. He does not believe these claims. Then she openly warns him: "If we are to be thrown much together, you had better believe it at once." They walk into the old brewery; there his gaze focuses on her white hand and he has the vague feeling that he has seen a similar hand on another person. Though he is tormented by her seeming unapproachability, Pip takes delight in his belief that Miss Havisham intends them for each other. They return to the waiting Miss Havisham. She informs Pip that Jaggers has arrived on business and will return for dinner.

As in the early days, Pip pushes Miss Havisham's chair, making "the old slow circuit round about the ashes of the bridal feast;" Estella soon leaves to prepare herself for dinner, and immediately Miss Havisham throws her arms around Pip and draws his head near hers. She commands him to love Estella no matter what suffering he must endure; she repeats the word *"love"* so often that it sounds to him like a curse. In a passionate whisper, she gives her definition of the term:

> I'll tell you what real love is. It is blind devotion, unquestioning self-humiliation, utter submission, trust and belief against yourself and against the whole world, giving up your whole heart and soul to the smiter — as I did!

As she finishes, she rises from her chair and strikes at the air; Pip seats her, then recognizes the scent which signifies that Jaggers has arrived. Miss Havisham immediately composes herself, for she is as afraid of her lawyer as is everyone else. Despite interruptions by his guardian, Pip explains the reason for his presence; then he, Jaggers, Estella, and Sarah Pocket go to a fine dinner — leaving Miss Havisham, who has never been seen to eat or drink. At the meal Jaggers presides but also displays a "determined reticence;" he does not look at Estella, though she often looks "at him, with interest and curiosity, if not distrust. . . ." Afterwards, Sarah's envy of Pip leads her not to join the company in Miss Havisham's room. Pip, Jaggers, Estella, and Miss Havisham play cards, though Pip is distracted by Estella's beauty which has now been further enhanced by jewels which Miss Havisham put on her. The game continues until nine o'clock; then it is arranged that Pip will meet Estella's coach when she comes to London. Pip leaves and goes to the Blue Boar where his room adjoins that of Jaggers. All night Miss Havisham's command to love Estella rings in his ears. Then, "a burst of gratitude comes upon |him|, that she should be destined for |him|, once the blacksmith's boy." These emotions lead him to forget Joe, whom he has not even bothered to visit. Yesterday's tears of regret are quickly dried.

Commentary

To Pip, as to any snob, the unattainable has the greatest charm. From this chapter, the reader may derive two definitions of love, one stated and the other implied. Miss Havisham defines love as a blind and suffering total self-sacrifice; in effect, her devotion to that definition explains the fact that she no longer exists, but rather inhabits a deathlike world devoted to revenge for her emotional murder. For Pip, love is an emotion which symbolizes what he does not have; it is a negative quality never made positive by any sexual response to Estella's beauty. She is inaccessible — thus providing in his search for access a motivation for most of the novel's action. The reader must recognize that Pip's definition of love is at least as sterile as Miss Havisham's.

CHAPTER 30

Summary

At breakfast the next morning, Pip tells Jaggers that he doubts "Orlick's being the right sort of man to fill a post of trust at Miss Havisham's." He is surprised that Jaggers agrees and says he will see that the porter is fired immediately. Since Pip does not want to meet Pumblechook, he decides to walk part of the way to London and Jaggers will have the coachman stop when they overtake him. To keep from seeing Pumblechook, Pip makes a point of avoiding the area around his place of business; he finds the old town interesting and is obviously flattered that many people suddenly recognize and stare after him.

Soon, however, Fate throws in his way "that unlimited miscreant, Trabb's boy;" Pip decides that "a serene and unconscious contemplation of him would best beseem |himself|, and would be most likely to quell his evil mind." The boy proves too much, however. First, he staggers off the road, teeth chattering and with every mark of humiliation, and pretends "to be in a paroxysm of terror and contrition, occasioned by the dignity of |Pip's| appearance." Though it is hard to bear the insult, Pip passes and within two hundred yards notes that Trabb's boy has circled and is approaching him a second time. The boy acts again as if shocked by Pip's greatness; he staggers "round and round |Pip| with knees more afflicted, and with uplifted hands as if beseeching for mercy." A crowd of spectators begins to observe his behavior with great joy. Again Pip passes, but soon sees the boy approaching for the third time; this time the prankster, imitating Pip, is strolling "along the pavement towards |him| on the opposite side of the street, attended by a company of delighted young friends to whom he from time to time exclaimed, with a wave of his hand, 'Don't know yah!' " After they pass, Trabb's boy turns on the now utterly deflated Pip; he chases him across a bridge and makes rude remarks — leaving him really nothing to do but endure the disgrace before his townspeople. The coach arrives, but by the time Pip reaches London the memory of the degrading spectacle has completely depressed him. He sends "a penitential codfish and barrel of oysters to Joe" in a weak attempt to compensate his conscience for not having visited; then he writes a vicious letter to Trabb which cuts off all potential business they might have had because of the clothier's so far forgetting "what he owed to the best interests of society, as to employ a boy who excited Loathing in every respectable mind."

At Barnard's Inn, Pip confesses to Herbert that he loves Estella and is much surprised that Herbert has known of his love since first meeting Pip in London. Pip acknowledges that he has done nothing to raise himself in life, that fortune alone has raised him. Now his recent meeting with Estella has raised a doubt: What if his luck should change and Miss Havisham lose interest in him? Herbert comforts him, saying: "The thing is settled and done, or Mr. Jaggers would not be in it." In addition, Herbert suggests that Estella's behavior and her known relationship to Miss Havisham raise doubts as to the wisdom of Pip's devotion: "Now, Handel, I am quite free from the flavour of sour grapes, upon my soul and honour! Not being bound to her |Estella|, can you not detach yourself from her?" Pip responds by saying that this is impossible; then the subject changes to Herbert's own romantic involvement. Referring to his father, he comments that men often marry most unsuitably, the result being at times that their potential in the world either dissolves or is given up to domestic or financial necessity. Though his mother would not approve of the girl's inferior family station, Herbert is secretly engaged to a girl named Clara. Her father, now a retired invalid in London, was formerly a purser (that is, one who purchased food for passenger ships); he has a wicked temper and is characteristically domineering. Meekly, Herbert says he will marry only when he has money: "You *can't* marry, you know, while you're looking about you." The conversation finished, Pip and Herbert stand watching the fire. Suddenly Pip notices in his pocket a playbill for Wopsle's play. After Herbert promises him that he shall soon meet Clara, they set out together for the theater and Wopsle's *Hamlet*.

Commentary

Before the meeting with Trabb's boy, Pip's sufferings with respect to the lower class have been self-inflicted pangs of conscience usually related to his treatment of Joe and Biddy. When he had himself been a member of that class, Estella's remarks were externally inflicted — but they came from above. Once he became a "gentleman," such suffering inflicted by his former townsmen, i.e., Mrs. Joe, Wopsle, the Hubbles, Pumblechook, suddenly ceased. This fact led him to consider himself vulnerable only from the perspective of Satis House; his false front is — he thinks — adequate protection from those below. Trabb's boy is the first member of his former class to assert that Pip's position as gentleman is a flimsy pose. In committing the outrages, Trabb's boy makes a sacrifice impossible for Wopsle and Pumblechook; he sacrifices both the goodwill of a valuable connection and (potentially) money. In writing the vicious letter to the boy's employer, Pip acts true to the ethic of his class; he cannot defend himself and must simply endure at the moment of the outrage (as he admits afterwards). Only money is a possible weapon; thus it is thematically consistent that Pip (in conversation with Herbert) would worry about a possible end to his luck and money, two elements now united in his view.

CHAPTER 31

Summary

The production of *Hamlet* with Wopsle (who now calls himself Waldengarver) in the role of the Danish prince is ludicrous. A major portion of the audience's amazement (or disgust) is directed toward Wopsle: "whenever that undecided Prince had to ask a question or state a doubt, the public helped him out with it." Peals of laughter greet his every action. Pip and Herbert finally give up their attempts to applaud him and join in the merriment. At the conclusion of the performance, they try to escape, but Wopsle has seen them and sends an attendant to invite them to his dressing room. They accept and soon view a grotesquely comic scene in which Wopsle, perspiring abundantly, is trying to remove his stocking in the presence of the man in charge of costumes, who fears that Wopsle is going to burst them. To Wopsle's question as to the effectiveness of his performance, Herbert — followed by Pip — responds that it was "massive and concrete." Apparently blind to the ridiculous production, Wopsle explains the audience response: "My view is a little classic and thoughtful for them here; but they will improve, they will improve." He further adds that the man in the gallery who most "cast derision" on his performance was paid by an envious actor who played Claudius in the production. Pip has pity for his self-deluding townsman. He and Herbert sympathetically invite Wopsle to dinner. In a dream that evening Pip associates the obviously high expectations of Wopsle for a great acting career with his own great expectations.

CHAPTER 32

Summary

One day as Pip is busy with his books he receives a brief note from Estella, saying that she is coming to London and that she writes in obedience to Miss Havisham, who wishes Pip to meet her coach. Pip's excitement causes him to have no rest or peace until the day arrives. He goes to the coach office four hours early. By chance, during his wait, Wemmick appears on his way to interview a client at Newgate Prison, and Pip decides the long wait could best be spent by accompanying him on the errand. The prison is dismal, and depressing; Pip notes that Wemmick, who is apparently popular and who takes "the familiar department of Mr. Jaggers' business," walks "among the prisoners, much as a gardener might walk among his plants." Pip hears several of the conversations, all carried on in Wemmick's totally impersonal way. Wemmick says the clients will ask him anything — but they will never direct questions to Jaggers. He explains that a great part of Jaggers' effectiveness comes from his self-assumed position:

> He's always so high. His constant height is of a piece with his immense abilities . . . Then, between his height and them, he slips in his subordinate . . . and so he has 'em, soul and body.

Pip returns to the coach office for a wait of three hours; there he thinks of Jaggers and of his own experience — how from the early times in the marshes to the present he has been strangely "encompassed by all this taint of prison and crime." He contrasts the unpleasantness of his visit to Newgate Prison with the beauty of Estella; then, as the coach approaches, he feels utterly contaminated. Estella waves from the coach window, and Pip has the vague feeling that he has seen a glimpse of the same face elsewhere.

CHAPTER 33

Summary

To Pip, Estella is "more delicately beautiful" than she had ever seemed; her manner toward him is also warmer, yet he senses "Miss Havisham's influence in the change." He is to take her to a part of London called Richmond, where she is to live at great expense with a lady who has the power to introduce her to society. Pip, encouraged by Estella's holding his arm and by her radiant warmth, says that he is as happy in the Pocket household as he could be anywhere away from her. Estella takes little notice of the comment and suggests that Matthew is superior to the rest of the Pockets; those jealous relatives, she remarks, are so envious of Pip that they have done everything possible to lower him in Miss Havisham's estimation. Estella assures him that their attempts fail and adds that she too has endured their false sympathy:

> You were not brought up in that strange house from a mere baby.— I was. You had not your little wits sharpened by their intriguing against you, suppressed and defenseless, under the mask of sympathy and pity and what not, that is soft and soothing.— I had.

Estella thanks Pip for drawing the relatives' attention away from her; she further gives him her hand and permits him to kiss her cheek. Then (to his dismay) she returns to that tone which implies that they are mere puppets enduring a forced relationship.

In the coach to Richmond they pass Newgate Prison, and Pip, who pretends at first not to recognize the place, answers Estella's questions by saying that Jaggers "has the reputation of being more in the secrets of that dismal place than any man in London." Estella answers that Jaggers is in on the secrets of every place. Pip cannot avoid recognizing that Estella means to win him; she tells him his name has been mentioned to the lady in Richmond and that he is welcome to visit her. She is to report to Miss Havisham often about the events of her stay. Near the end of the trip she (for the first time) quite consciously calls Pip by his first name, knowing the way he will treasure that familiarity. He leaves her at the elegant old house and (before returning to Matthew Pocket's) reflects on the irony of his and Estella's relationship:

> And still I stood looking at the house, thinking how happy I should be if I lived there with her, and knowing that I never was happy with her, but always miserable.

CHAPTER 34

Summary

As Pip has grown accustomed to his expectations, he has begun to notice their effect on himself and those about him. The effect on himself he disguises, for his conscience is in a state of "chronic uneasiness" concerning his neglect of Joe and Biddy. At times he thinks that it would be better had he never met Miss Havisham and that "there was no fire like the forge fire and the kitchen fire at home." Both he and Herbert fall into debt through senseless extravagance; at Startop's suggestion they join a club called the Finches of the Grove, whose members (including Drummle) do nothing but argue and dine expensively. Debt depresses Herbert, who is too proud to accept over-generosity from Pip and who cannot himself afford their style of living. Spending part of his time at Richmond and more of it at Barnard's Inn and at the Pockets', Pip begins to spend money as a way of forgetting misery, a habit which Herbert also adopts: "There was a gay fiction among us that we were constantly enjoying ourselves, and a skeleton truth that we never did." In order to feel they are making some attempt to meet financial obligations, they make elaborate lists of debts, then leave a margin for subsequent expenses. The margin is soon spent and extended, but the bookkeeping procedure gives them a feeling of security and accomplishment. One evening a letter is dropped through a slit in the door; it is from Trabb and informs Pip that Mrs. Joe is dead and that his attendance is requested at the burial on the following Monday.

CHAPTER 35

Summary

This is the first relative's death which Pip has faced. His response is not one of tenderness toward his sister; rather he feels a "shock of regret" and a "violent indignation against the assailant from whom she had suffered so much." He offers consolation to Joe in a letter, then arrives at his old home for the burial on Monday. Memories of the past flood his consciousness as he walks about. He is disgusted by the false mood generated by the funeral director Trabb. All the townspeople admire the dismal atmosphere. Joe is also aware of the vulgarity of the scene: he whispers to Pip that he would prefer to carry

> . . . her to the church [himself], along with three or four friendly ones wot come to it with willing harts and arms, but it were considered wot the neighbors would look down on such and would be of opinions as it were wanting in respect.

Trabb orders everyone to get out handkerchiefs and prepare for the march, which the neighbors obviously approve. Pumblechook insists all during the procession on arranging Pip's hat band and smoothing his cloak; the excessive pride of the Hubbles, "surpassingly conceited and vainglorious in being members of so distinguished a procession," is equally repulsive to the already depressed Pip. At last Mrs. Joe is laid to rest.

They return to the cottage, and when all have left except Joe and Biddy, "the house felt wholesomer." There is no ease in the meal, however. Joe obviously (for Pip's benefit) tries to use manners which are foreign to him. Pip ask Joe if he may sleep the night in his old room and feels that he has "done rather a great thing in making the request." Towards evening he walks into the garden with Biddy; she tells him of Mrs. Joe's death, of her necessity to leave Joe's household and her plans to be a schoolmistress, and of Orlick's last appearance standing nearby on the night of Mrs. Joe's death (Orlick is still pursuing Biddy). Biddy tells Pip she saw Orlick just a moment ago watch them, and Pip says he "would spend any money or take any pains to drive |Orlick| out of that country." Pip then turns a self-righteous anger on Biddy: he reproaches her for not believing that he will visit Joe often and is angry at her for calling him "Mr. Pip." There is a coolness between them after this. Pip goes to bed and there reflects on "what an unkindness, what an injury, what an injustice, Biddy had done |him|." Next morning he warmly parts with Joe; to Biddy he says while shaking her hand: "I am not angry, but I am hurt." As he walks away, the mists are rising; they suggest to him that Biddy was correct: he will not return for a long while.

CHAPTER 36

Summary

As time passes, Herbert and Pip go from bad to worse with respect to their financial affairs. With anticipation Pip awaits his coming of age, his twenty-first birthday; and on the day before its arrival he receives an official note from Wemmick, informing him that Jaggers "would be glad if |he| would call upon him at five in the afternoon of the auspicious day." Jaggers congratulates him but does not (as he anticipated) make known the name of his benefactor. Rather, he tells him that he is living extravagantly, that he is in debt to an extent of which he is probably unaware, and that from this time forth he must take his financial matters into his own hands, living on five hundred pounds each year until the appearance of his benefactor. Jaggers says it may be years before the benefactor is revealed to Pip, and he again reminds him that his function is as a mere agent being paid for his services. When the identity of the benefactor is revealed, Jaggers' part in the affair will be concluded. The interview closed, Pip invites his guardian to dinner and goes to wait for him in Wemmick's office. While there, he asks Wemmick for advice as to how he could help a friend achieve commercial success; Wemmick is opposed to any such action, for he is now in his unemotional office pose. Thus Pip asks if his home personality may present a less callous view; Wemmick confirms the possibility and says to Pip of Walworth: "You will be welcome there, in a private and personal capacity." Dinner is unpleasant; the twenty-first birthday hardly seems worthwhile in such a "guarded and suspicious world" as Jaggers makes of it. Pip is "intensely melancholy" and, after the lawyer's departure, Herbert relates that Jaggers made him too feel "dejected and guilty."

CHAPTER 37

Summary

Pip decides to go to Wemmick's home at Walworth on Sunday. On arriving, he is welcomed by the Aged, who tells him that Wemmick expects Pip but is away briefly. The Aged informs Pip that Wemmick had begun his career in the law after having been prepared for a career in a winery; he adds that after his own deafness came on, his son took charge of him and "by little and little made out this elegant and beautiful property." The one-sided conversation is interrupted by the arrival of Wemmick, who is accompanied by a lady friend named Miss Skiffins. Pip judges the lady to be two or three years younger than Wemmick and "to stand possessed of portable property;" he notes that she is "of a wooden appearance, and was, like her escort, in the post-office branch of the service." Her actions demonstrate that she is a frequent visitor and that she has high regard for the Aged. Soon Wemmick suggests that he show Pip how the island looks in winter. They walk about and Pip takes the opportunity to find out Wemmick's private sentiments on his helping Herbert. Pip relates the whole history of his relations with Herbert and his family. He confesses they might all have done better without his great expectations, and expresses his wish to contribute secretly about a hundred pounds a year "to keep |Herbert| in good hope and heart — and gradually to buy him on to some small partnership." In a private capacity Wemmick agrees to help him. They return and sit down to tea with the Aged and Miss Skiffins, while the Aged reads aloud to them from a newspaper. During the reading, Pip notes that on occasion Wemmick steals his arm around Miss Skiffins' waist — only to have her firmly remove it.

Pip soon leaves, but within a week he receives a note from Wemmick saying some progress has been made on Herbert's business. A worthy shipping broker named Clarriker had been found who was "not long established in business, who wanted intelligent help, and who wanted capital, and who in due course of time and receipt would want a partner." Clarriker had agreed to employ Herbert for a time before accepting him as a partner and to keep Pip's part in the arrangement secret. Sometime later a radiant Herbert approaches Pip, telling him that his opening has come at last (with Clarriker). After seeing Herbert's pleasure, Pip goes to bed and cries "to think that |his| expectations had done some good to somebody."

CHAPTER 38

Summary

Though Pip visits Estella in Richmond, even more often "the unquiet spirit" within him haunts the house where she stays. Mrs. Brandley, the woman with whom she lives, had been a friend of Miss Havisham's before the time of her seclusion; neither she nor Estella feels a close tie with the other, but the understanding is established that they are necessary to each other. From Estella Pip receives every kind of torture; he is placed "on terms of familiarity |but not| on terms of favour." She treats him either as a near relative or brother, or she makes of him a tool to tease her other admirers (of whom there are many). Her tone employed with him varies: at times she speaks in a way which suggests their relationship is a forced one, but at others she seems to pity him. One evening she says: "Pip, Pip, will you never take warning?" She requests on numerous occasions that he accompany her to Satis House. The first of these visits is particularly shocking to him. Miss Havisham appears "more dreadfully fond of Estella" than he has ever noted; she hangs on the girl's every word. Through Miss Havisham's questioning of him and of Estella, Pip sees reflected "the intensity of a mind mortally hurt and diseased" so as to receive its only pleasure from a vicarious revenge on all men. It is little consolation to Pip that he believes Miss Havisham intends Estella for him, since he must spend the interval watching his intended bride giving insane pleasure to the inhabitant of a "darkened and unhealthy house."

Miss Havisham is not completely pleased with her creation, however. One evening Pip watches Estella remove herself from her foster mother's fondling and hears her say she is tired of herself. An argument follows; Miss Havisham accuses Estella of being an ingrate and of being utterly cold even towards her. Estella responds that she is only what Miss Havisham has made her; her pride and hardness are characteristics which Miss Havisham once applauded, and now they are an unalterable nature which is directed toward every person whom she meets (including her foster mother). Throughout the scene, even with the old woman moaning and obviously hurt, Estella remains indifferent, unemotionl, and logical; she can neither understand nor experience feeling since she has been taught that it will destroy her as it did Miss Havisham.

Pip leaves the room, his last view revealing Estella as she has stood throughout the scene and a crushed Miss Havisham lying helpless on the floor "among the other bridal wrecks." In depression he walks about the ruined grounds, then returns to find the two women reconciled. For the first time he spends the night at Satis House, but he rests badly. The day's experiences have so unnerved him that he gets up for a walk late in the night; outside in a passageway he sees Miss Havisham walking slowly "in a ghostly manner, making a low cry." He follows her. The cry never ceases as she moves toward "the mildewed air of the feast-chamber." He leaves — but throughout the night hears footsteps and the continuous low cry. Pip and Estella leave the next day. He never on subsequent visits sees a renewal of the argument between the two women, but he senses that "something like fear" implants itself with Miss Havisham's other characteristics.

A few days after the return to London, Pip attends a meeting of the Finches of the Grove. Various ladies are being toasted, and Pip is shocked when Drummle proposes a toast to Estella of Richmond. In anger, he accuses Drummle of toasting a lady he does not know, but when next day Drummle delivers a note in Estella's handwriting, Pip is forced to apologize. He is greatly pained "that Estella should show any favour to a contemptible, clumsy, sulky booby, so very far below the average." Moreover, he soon finds that Drummle is pursuing Estella closely, and though she treats him like her other suitors, he is a Spider "used to lying in wait" and has the patience of his kind. When Pip confronts Estella with the subject, she answers: "Moths, and all sorts of ugly creatures hover about a lighted candle. Can the candle help it?" She further adds that she deceives and entraps many men; only with Pip is she honest.

Commentary

While emphasis on Pip's pride, unhappiness, and pursuit of Estella recur throughout the chapter, another major emphasis is introduced for the first time. Previously it has appeared that Miss Havisham had successfully created a deathlike world in which she is unaffected by the pangs of emotional distress. With all clocks stopped at the hour of her emotional collapse, she relives and preserves that moment of greatest suffering — thus employing her total emotional force and leaving no capacity for feeling a later hurt. Pride's creations, however, have a way of turning on their creators. A major theme of nineteenth-century literature is the sin of *hubris* (pride), as exemplified in the scientist who sacrifices other human beings or human concerns in quest of his own goals (for example, Dr. Frankenstein, Dr. Rappaccini, etc.). Just as those scientists' obsessions lead them to fail to recognize that their creations will offer them no refuge, so Miss Havisham's sole concern for revenge (symbolized by her constructing an emotionless weapon from a human being) fails to reckon with the fact that the very coldness she has molded and praised in Estella will prevent the creation from ever having a more intense feeling — even for her foster mother. Estella thus causes Miss Havisham a second emotional crisis — and again Miss Havisham collapses.

CHAPTER 39

Summary

Pip is twenty-three; he has concluded his studies with Mr. Pocket (though he still reads regularly and remains on good terms with his former tutor) and now lives in the Temple of Garden Court, having left Barnard's Inn more than a year before. He still has heard nothing to enlighten him on the subject of his expectations. Pip, alone for a time since Herbert is in France on business, has sat down to read on a violently rainy evening which has capped a week of wretched weather. Concluding his reading at eleven o'clock, he puts his book aside and suddenly, through the sounds of the storm, hears a foodstep on the stairs. Some nervous response makes him connect the sound with his dead sister, but he recovers himself and, when he hears the footstep stumble, takes the reading lamp to the head of the staircase. The man calls for Mr. Pip and, when he approaches, looks at Pip "with an incomprehensible air of being touched and pleased by the sight of [him]." The man appears to be a sea voyager of about sixty. He has long, iron-grey hair and is a muscular man who has been browned and hardened by exposure to the weather. In amazement, Pip sees that he is holding out his hands to him in recognition. A moment later the man states disappointment at not being recognized himself. Shocked by a question as to whether there is anyone near, Pip becomes irritated; then he recognizes the stranger: it is his convict from the marshes. Pip reluctantly shakes his hand, tells him he hopes he has mended his ways, suggests that no thanks for an act so long ago are necessary, and warns him that his own new station in life makes their ways incompatibly different. Then Pip offers him a drink and is amazed to see tears in the convict's eyes. Because of this, Pip is softened, feeling a touch of guilt, and apologizes to the convict for his abruptness. The convict then tells him that he has made a great fortune as "a sheep-farmer, stock-breeder, other trades besides, away in the new world." Pip's interest in the success story is obviously not great; he immediately reminds the convict of the two pound notes he sent, then tries to pay them back — only to have the convict burn them. Then Pip is asked how he came to his good furtune. During Pip's reply, the convict interrupts and reveals his knowledge of all the details of Pip's arrangement.

Pip suddenly knows the truth: the convict is his benefactor. In a state of shock, Pip begins to faint, but the convict catches him. As he is approached, Pip shudders and listens to the explanation:

> Yes, Pip, dear boy, I've made a gentleman on you! . . . I tell
> it, fur you to know as that there hunted hunghill dog wot you
> kep life in, got his head so high that he could make a gentle-
> man — and, Pip, you're him.

Pip could not have felt more horrified if the man had been a beast; yet
he continues to listen: "Pip, I'm your second father. You're my
son — more to me nor any son. I've put away money, only for you to
spend." All through his hardships, the man had thought of nothing but
the boy on the marshes who saved him. He planned to make of the boy
a gentleman if he ever achieved liberty and money. He admires Pip's
jewelry, his clothes, and the books he reads; his elation at the success of
his creation blinds him to Pip's negative reactions. When asked if there
is a lady he loves, Pip thinks passionately of Estella. The convict says
that if she cannot be had by the mere winning, then money will back
him in the pursuit.

As Pip thinks how much happier he would have been had he never
left the forge, he hears the man say his life has been one of anticipa-
tion — waiting for this very moment when he would make himself
known to the blacksmith become gentleman. The man faced his own
dismal situation by thinking: "If I ain't a gentleman, nor yet ain't got
no learning, I'm the owner of such." The convict risked everything in
coming to Pip. He had been sent away from England for life, and he
says of his return: " It is death to come back. There's been overmuch
coming back of late years, and I should of a certainty be hanged if
took." Pip now realizes that not only have the bubbles of his aspirations burst before his eyes, he is also bound to protect the man he
abhors. The convict goes to bed and Pip views the wreck of his own life:

> Miss Havisham's intentions toward me, all a mere dream;
> Estella not designed for me; I only suffered in Satis House as a
> convenience, a sting for the greedy relations, a model with a
> mechanical heart to practice on when no other practice was at
> hand; . . . it was for the convict . . . that I had deserted Joe.

Pip now needs the comfort he could derive from the simplicity and
faithfulness of Joe and Biddy, but he realizes he can never undo what
he has done. This is the end of the second stage of Pip's expectations.

Commentary

For the reader, this chapter poses more questions than it offers
answers; the principal one of these concerns the avenue Pip will follow
now that his expectations are (in terms of his pride) demolished. A par-

tial answer has been provided by the novel's structure, especially if one considers Pip and Estella to be parallel characters. Their similarity is established in the following ways: (1) both are orphans practically from birth; (2) both develop an unemotional hardness from the environments into which they are thrown (i.e., Miss Havisham's teaching and the convict's money); (3) both are deprived of a regular childhood (Estella, physically, by the walls of Satis House, and Pip by the harshness of his treatment by Mrs. Joe and her associates); (4) both are tools used to compensate for another's lack of fulfilment (Estella for Miss Havisham's revenge, Pip for the convict's social aspirations); (5) both are influenced beyond their awareness by crime (Estella by her father and by her mother's wildness, though the reader does not yet know this, and Pip by the convict); (6) both are unable to respond with love to foster parents who have presented them with financial security; and (7) both are arrogantly proud. However, there are certain crucial differences between the two: Pip, unlike Estella, is always conscience-plagued because he judges what he has become against a moral standard symbolized by Joe and the forge; Estella, on the other hand, has seen only the one world which Miss Havisham created for her, and that is a world without morality, and in which pride, arrogance, insensitivity, and suspicion are virtues. For this reason, Estella not only cannot reciprocate with her foster parent a feeling of love; she cannot even understand the sentiment she is witnessing in another. Ironically, a second contrast concerns self-awareness: Estella (through her frequent warnings to Pip and her argument with Miss Havisham) demonstrates a self-awareness which has no illusory expectations of happiness. By contrast, Pip's pose fools him as much or even more than it fools others; only on infrequent occasions before the appearance of his benefactor (such as the prodding by Trabb's boy) has he realized his own pretensions.

SUMMARY OF IMPORTANT DEVELOPMENTS

1. Pip becomes established in London with Mr. Jaggers as his tutor, Mr. Matthew Pocket as his director of studies, and Herbert Pocket as a congenial companion and friend.

2. The struggle in Pip's mind between his duty to Joe and his personal ambition continues, though self-interest dominates his generous impulses, and the devotion to Estella remains a powerful factor in his life.

3. We find that the fortunes of the Pocket family comprise a subplot well integrated with the main theme of Pip's great expectations.

4. Parallel romances to Pip's dreams of Estella are Herbert's love for Clara, and Wemmick's courting of Miss Skiffins.

5. We meet Molly, the mysterious housekeeper of Mr. Jaggers.

6. Whenever Pip meets Estella, he sees in her face the ghost of some strange familiarity to someone he has known.

7. Up to the crisis, there is reason to assume that Miss Havisham is Pip's benefactress.

8. Estella is sent to Mrs. Brandley to acquire polish and meet society. There is a complication in her tolerance of the unsavory Drummle.

9. Pip and Herbert fall into debt in London.

10. Mrs. Joe dies as the result of her mysterious attack by an unknown assailant.

11. Pip decides to help Herbert as a result of his own good fortune.

12. A week after Pip's twenty-third birthday, the convict appears with the news that he, and not Miss Havisham, is the young man's benefactor.

13. This intelligence removes Estella still farther from Pip's sphere, and fills him with remorse when he thinks of leaving Joe for so wretched a man.

14. A new problem arises in the necessity for protecting the returned convict from the law which enforces hanging as the penalty for life transports who come back to England.

Stage III of Pip's Great Expectations

CHAPTER 40

Summary

Pip realizes the impossibility of keeping the convict safe in his quarters. He decides to eliminate suspicions by his announcing in the morning that his uncle has unexpectedly come from the country. Suddenly realizing he has no light, he goes to the neighboring lodge and gets a watchman to bring a lantern. As he gropes down the bleak staircase, he falls over a man crouching in the corner, whom he cannot identify. The man will not give his name, and by the time Pip returns with the lantern and watchman, he has escaped — still unidentified. A conversation with the watchman reveals that when Pip's "uncle" entered he had been followed by a man who wore "a dust-colored kind of clothes" under a dark coat; the watchman had thought them to be together.

Back in his chamber, Pip is told that his benefactor's real name is Magwitch but that he is using the name Provis. When he came to the chamber, he had brought no one with him; then he adds: "But I think there *was* a person, too, come in alonger me." Magwitch says he is not known in London and that Jaggers had been his lawyer at an earlier trial. Pip loses his appetite by watching the way in which Magwitch eats; to Pip he looks "terribly like a hungry old dog." Finally Magwitch gets up from the table, congratulates Pip on being a "genuine" gentleman, and says his only concern is that he be permitted to stand by and watch the gentleman he has created. He throws a thick pocketbook on the table, saying his pleasure will be "to see my gentleman spend his money *like* a gentleman." "Almost in a frenzy of fear and dislike," Pip stops Magwitch's monologue and begins to consider how the fugitive can best be kept safe. Magwitch apologizes for being "low," for discussing money and his own intended pleasures, and adds that the danger of his planning to stay permanently is minimized by the fact that he is known only by Pip, Jaggers, and Wemmick. As to where and how he shall live, he turns these considerations over to Pip. Pip decides to find a room for Magwitch (whom he now calls Provis) nearby: it can be occupied on Herbert's arrival, which is expected in two or three days. It is decided that the best dress for Magwitch will be that of a prosperous farmer. While Pip is securing clothes and renting space nearby, Magwitch is to remain in the chambers and open the door on no account.

Pip goes about his errands. He also visits Jaggers to assure himself that all Magwitch has told him is true. He confesses his having thought Miss Havisham to be his benefactress; Jaggers, in denying responsibility for that, tells Pip: "Take nothing on its looks; take everything on evidence. There's no better rule." Then he relates his experience with Magwitch and, while refusing to be told outright, denies that his former client is now in England. Pip shakes hands with Jaggers, and as he leaves he notices that his guardian's eyes are looking closely at him. Returning home, he finds Provis drinking rum and smoking. Next day the clothes arrive, and Pip notes that the better he dresses Provis,

> . . . the more he looked like the slouching fugitive on the marshes . . . The influences of his solitary hut-life were upon him besides, and gave him a savage air that no dress could tame; added to these were the influences of his subsequent branded life among men, and, crowning all, his consciousness that he was dodging and hiding now.

To Pip the man is a mystery, and "every hour so increased [his] abhorrence of him." After about five days, Herbert arrives in a jolly mood; he suddenly stops, however, when he sees Provis (who is handling a knife he had drawn and getting out a worn Bible). At Pip's urging, Herbert swears secrecy on Provis' Bible; then he shakes hands with the fugitive.

CHAPTER 41

Summary

Pip reveals the secret to Herbert and sees his own feelings reflected in his friend's face, especially his disgust for Magwitch. Herbert and Pip principally take offense at Magwitch's revealing a sense of triumph in Pip's rise; the fugitive "had no perception of the possibility of [Pip's] finding any fault with [his] good fortune." Again, Magwitch apologizes for being "low" and promises to put "a gen-teel muzzle on." After Herbert and Pip take him to his quarters, they return, and Pip experiences "the first moment of relief [he] had known since the night of [Magwitch's] arrival." Pip and Herbert discuss the situation: Magwitch wants Pip to spend more money (for "horses, and carriages, and lavish appearances of all kinds"); Pip is in debt and prepared for no profession; and there is no hope of repaying Magwitch what he has already spent, though, of course, he can spend no more. Both recognize that if Pip disappoints Magwitch, the fugitive's unfulfilled hopes will likely lead him to give himself up to the authorities. They agree that the best plan is for Pip to accompany Magwitch in an escape from England; then a break can be made. At the appointed time Magwitch arrives for breakfast. Pip then asks him to tell about himself and the individual with whom he fought long ago in the marshes. Magwitch, claiming that "wotever I done, is worked out and paid for," demands that Herbert swear secrecy again before the story is related.

CHAPTER 42

Summary

Magwitch relates his story, which he says can best be summarized as follows:

> In jail and out of jail, in jail and out of jail, in jail and out of jail. There, you've got it. That's *my* life pretty much, down to such times as I got shipped off, arter Pip stood my friend.

He knows neither his parents nor the circumstances and place of his birth. His first memory is of stealing turnips for his living in Essex. As a young boy, his appearance frightened everyone, and soon it became a general conclusion that he was "hardened." "Tramping, begging, thieving, working sometimes:" these were his primary occupations from childhood to manhood, and none of them paid well, while all were quick to get a man in trouble. About twenty years ago at Epsom races, he met a man named Compeyson who was well-educated, smooth-talking, handsome, and in general, had set himself up for a gentleman. (Compeyson, whom Magwitch hates, was the other convict whom Pip had seen in the marshes and with whom Magwitch had fought.) Compeyson took Magwitch on as a partner in business; his business was "swindling, handwriting, forging, stolen bank-note passing, and suchlike." Another partner of Compeyson was a man in poor health whose name was Arthur; he and Compeyson had made "a pot of money" by defrauding a rich lady, but Compeyson had gambled it away. The dying Arthur lived with Compeyson, and the latter kept a careful "account agen him for board and lodging, in case he should ever get better to work it out." The night Arthur died Magwitch saw him come raving to Compeyson, talking of a woman with a shroud who was all in white and who had blood spots over her heart because Compeyson had broken it.

Soon Magwitch's business dealings had become so dangerous and his debt so great that Compeyson had him in "such nets as made |him| his black slave." For a minor crime done at the bidding of Compeyson, Magwitch alone was jailed. Later they were both committed for a felony, and Compeyson insisted that they be tried separately rather than together. Compeyson's lawyers made much of his background and appearance; such was not possible for Magwitch:

> And when the verdict come, warn't it Compeyson as was recommended to mercy on account of good character and bad company, and giving up all the information he could agen me, and warn't it me as got never a word but Guilty?

At that time, since Compeyson's sentence was seven years and Magwitch's fourteen, Magwitch had threatened the coward Compeyson that he would have revenge. They were on the same prison ship, but only once was Magwitch able to attack his enemy; that time he succeeded in scarring his face before order was restored. Soon after that event Magwitch escaped and was hiding among the graves when Pip approached. Next day, through Pip, he found that Compeyson also had escaped and was on the marshes, and he saw to it, even by sacrificing his own freedom, that his hated adversary was captured. At the escape trial, Compeyson again received a light sentence, while Magwitch "was put in irons, brought to trial again, and sent for life." Magwitch knows nothing of Compeyson's present whereabouts. At the conclusion of Magwitch's monologue, Herbert passes a note to Pip which reads: "Young Havisham's name was Arthur. Compeyson is the man who professed to be Miss Havisham's lover."

CHAPTER 43

Summary

Much of Pip's shrinking from Magwitch may be traced to Estella; he reflects "on the abyss between Estella in her pride and beauty, and the returned transport whom [he] harboured." A new fear comes over Pip with respect to Compeyson, who he recognizes must live in mortal fear of Magwitch and would take any opportunity to rid himself of the threat. He decides he must see Estella and Miss Havisham, though he decides to tell the former nothing of Magwitch. He goes to Mrs. Brandley's and is surprised to find that Estella has gone to Satis House (for she never goes there without him). On the pretence that he has a binding promise to visit Joe, Pip leaves Magwitch for a brief visit to Satis House. When he arrives at the Blue Boar, the first person he sees is Bentley Drummle. Each pretends not to see the other. Drummle lets it be known that later he is dining with Estella, and, as tempers flare, he baits Pip: "But don't lose your temper. Haven't you lost enough without that?" Mutually deciding they are no longer on speaking terms, they leave the coffee room. Pip watches Drummle mount his horse and is suddenly surprised by the appearance of his attendant: "The slouching shoulders, and ragged hair, of this man, whose back was towards me, reminded me of Orlick." Pip is too upset to verify his observation; thus he washes and sets out for Miss Havisham's.

CHAPTER 44

Summary

At Satis House Pip finds Estella and Miss Havisham together. The look they exchange on his arrival reveals their awareness that a change has taken place in him. As Miss Havisham, at first confused, begins to look steadily at him, he delivers his monologue: he is now as unhappy as she could ever have intended; he knows his patron and that the relationship will never bring to him "station, fortune, anything." From Miss Havisham, he learns that Jaggers' connection with both her and his patron is a coincidence. She made use of the situation to torment her relations; "kindness" is no necessity for one who has suffered as she. She adds: "You made your own snares; *I* never made them." Pip then turns the conversation to her family; he tells her that she deeply wrongs "both Mr. Matthew Pocket and his son Herbert, if [she] suppose[s] them to be otherwise than generous, upright, open, and incapable of anything designing or mean." Pip's contrasting Matthew's family with her other relations "seemed . . . to do them good" with Miss Havisham. When she asks what she can do for them, Pip mentions the service he has secretly performed for Herbert and lets it be known that his ability to continue that service is blocked by his awareness of the source of his expectations. There is a long silence; then Miss Havisham looks up and asks what else she can do. Pip turns to Estella's "unmoved countenance;" he confesses his love for her, suggests that the confession would have come earlier had he not believed them destined for each other by Miss Havisham, and admits that he no longer has hopes of winning her. He does not accuse Miss Havisham of sheer cruel design: "I think that in the endurance of her own trial, she forgot mine, Estella." Estella calmly declares that she cannot understand the sentiments of which he speaks; she can only define love abstractly, for it corresponds to "nothing in [her] breast." She adds that she had tried to warn him, and that she is to marry Drummle. Pip, in agony, drops his face into his hands; looking up, he notices "such a ghastly look upon Miss Havisham's [face] that it impressed [him], even in [his] passionate hurry and grief." He pleads with Estella to give herself to someone more worthy than Drummle, but she answers that the choice is her own — made because she is tired of her present life and because she would not give herself to a sensitive man "who would the soonest feel (if people do feel such things) that I took nothing to him" Though she calls Pip a "visionary boy — or man" and adds that he will get over his love for her, he vows that she will be forever a part of his life.

Pip, the narrator who years later recalls these emotions, considers his impressions at the time of his departure:

> But ever afterwards, I remembered — and soon afterwards with stronger reason — that while Estella looked at me merely with incredulous wonder, the spectral figure of Miss Havisham, her hand still covering her breast, seemed all resolved into a ghastly stare of pity and remorse.

After leaving the terrible scene, Pip walks all the way to London — realizing the emptiness of the moment: "All done, all gone!" After midnight he crosses London Bridge and proceeds to the Temple. At the gate he receives a brief note in Wemmick's handwriting which reads: "Don't go home."

Commentary

Pip's fate is made more pathetic by the events related in this chapter. Before this, the reader could consider Miss Havisham cruel and viciously revengeful, now he must admit — like Pip — that she is merely a disordered mind who acted not from cruelty, but rather from an insane distortion of values in which the presence of her own suffering made any other consideration impossible for her. The pathetic (Pip) falls victim to the pathetic (Miss Havisham): Dickens is not here drawing a hero-villainess relationship. Estella, who has no choice and fails to understand the emotions displayed by either Pip or Miss Havisham, is clearly the most pathetic. She can feel neither pain nor love; she endures rather than lives — and for this reason Dickens has throughout the novel associated her with imagery of inanimate objects.

CHAPTER 45

Summary

Pip accepts the warning and soon rents a cheap room for the night. It is an upsetting and long night in which he sleeps badly, if at all. The next morning he goes to see Wemmick at Walworth, where he finds (though Wemmick is reluctant to give explicit information) that his quarters at the Temple are being watched and that Compeyson is still alive and in London. Wemmick, without ever mentioning Provis' name, lets it be known that there had been danger, that to break from the city would have been a mistake, and that Magwitch had had to be moved to a safer place within the city. The best place was to the home of Clara, Herbert's fiancée, for it had an unoccupied top floor for rent and was the safest choice for three reasons: (1) it is out of the mainstream of London life; (2) Magwitch can be contacted by Herbert without Pip's going near him; and (3) it is near the river, where a boat would be readily available at any time that an escape is desirable. Through Herbert's efforts, the transfer of Magwitch had been taken care of by nine o'clock the previous evening. At the old lodging, it was understood that Pip's uncle had been summoned to Dover. Another advantage of Herbert's having carried the action out (according to Wemmick) is that it was done without the help of Pip; if anyone had been following his movements, Pip would have been far away at Satis House and thus missed the move. Wemmick is glad to have helped; he offers (from a Walworth point of view) any future help which might prove necessary, gives Pip the new address of Magwitch, and tells him it will be safe to visit there in the evening. After Wemmick leaves for work, Pip and the Aged spend the day asleep in front of the fire. Pip leaves after supper.

CHAPTER 46

Summary

By eight o'clock Pip approaches Mill Pond Bank, the area where Magwitch is hidden. Knocking on the door, he confronts "an elderly woman of a pleasant and thriving appearance," who is obviously the housekeeper. She is immediately replaced by Herbert, who silently leads Pip into the parlor, shuts the door, and tells him that all is well. Clara is upstairs with her father, Mr. Barley, a rum-drinking gout-stricken invalid who growls tyrannically. He lives in the past — weighing out family food rations as he had done on shipboard — and though he is Clara's only living relative, Herbert scornfully calls him Gruffandgrim. Mrs. Whimple, the pleasant lady who had met Pip at the door, is the only person aware of Clara's and Herbert's romance. As Pip and Herbert converse, there enters a charmingly pretty and dark-haired girl of about twenty who "might have passed for a captive fairy." It is Clara, whom Pip had not met before, and he is quite pleased by her gentleness, and by "something so confiding, loving, and innocent, in her modest manner of yielding herself to Herbert's embracing arm."

Suddenly Old Barley's growl and stomping are heard above, and Clara has to rush to serve him. She soon returns, and Herbert takes Pip upstairs to see Magwitch's quarters. To Pip his benefactor appears calm and comfortably settled. It even strikes him that the man is somewhat softened. Pip relates all of Wemmick's information and advice, though he does refrain — as he had previously determined — from mentioning that Compeyson is in London. Magwitch promises to keep himself hidden. Herbert plans the future escape from England: Pip is to acquire a boat and, while keeping it at the Temple, make it his habit to row about on the Thames. Later, since both he and Herbert are good oarsmen, they can row Magwitch to a place where he and Pip can safely board an outgoing steamer. Magwitch is elated by the plan. He also agrees that if he should see the boys rowing on the river he will not openly acknowledge them, but will pull down the window blind to show that all is well. As he parts with his benefactor, Pip is surprised by the new emotion he feels: "I little supposed my heart could ever be as heavy and anxious at parting from him as it was now." He also is impressed by the "redeeming youth and trust and hope" which overflow in Mrs. Whimple and Clara's household. He acquires his boat and begins rowing daily — though he "could not get rid of the notion of being watched."

CHAPTER 47

Summary

Several weeks pass with no change or sign from Wemmick. Pip's creditors press him, but he remains firm in his determination "that it would be a heartless fraud to take more money from |his| patron in the existing state of |his| uncertain thoughts and plans." An impression settles heavily upon him that Estella is married, but to avoid confirmation of it he neglects reading the newspapers. "Condemned to inaction and a state of constant restlessness and suspense," he passes the waiting time by often rowing in his boat. One evening after rowing and seeing Magwitch's signal that all is well, he decides to attend "the theatre where Mr. Wopsle had achieved his questionable triumph." As the comically hideous play is being performed, Pip notes that Mr. Wopsle is not only aware of his presence; rather the actor spends any time he is not delivering lines "staring in |Pip's| direction as if he were lost in amazement." Pip cannot understand this, and after the final curtain he finds Wopsle waiting for him at the door. Wopsle immediately asks Pip who was with him at the performance. Pip, alarmed, asks Wopsle to explain. The actor recalls the chase of the convicts long ago on the marshes and tells Pip that the prisoner who had been mauled in the face was sitting behind him in the theater, though he had left before Wopsle went offstage. Pip's sudden awareness that Compeyson had been behind him throws him into a "special and peculiar terror;" yet he disguises the emotion from Wopsle by pretending idle curiosity. Afterwards, they have refreshments together, and Pip arrives at the Temple after midnight. He relates the event to Herbert, and they decide to pass the information to Wemmick, to remind him that they are waiting for his hint as to a possible course of action, and to be even more cautious than they had been in the past.

CHAPTER 48

Summary

A week after the theater experience, Pip is suddenly overtaken by Jaggers (while strolling in Cheapside). He is invited to dinner and changes his intended excuse to an acceptance when he finds that Wemmick is also going to be there. They go first to Little Britain, where Jaggers is to close his office for the day; there Pip is unable to catch Wemmick's eye. He is given a note from Miss Havisham which requests that he come to Satis House on the business matter discussed at their previous meeting (Herbert's financial situation). At Wemmick's suggestion, Pip decides to make the trip the next day rather than write a formal reply. Jaggers mentions Estella: "So, Pip! Our friend the Spider has played his cards. He has won the pool." Painfully, Pip agrees, but Jaggers continues, saying "the stronger will win in the end |Drummle or Estella|, but the stronger has to be found out first." The choice is now a toss-up, Jaggers feels: "If he should turn to and beat her, he may possibly get the strength on his side; if it should be a question of intellect, he certainly will not." On hearing these words from Jaggers, Molly (the housekeeper) appears particularly upset: "the action of her fingers was like the action of knitting." Her eyes and hands recall to Pip the hands of one who had walked with him in the ruined garden at Satis House and the hand which had waved to him from the window of the coach; he feels "absolutely certain that this woman was Estella's mother." Jaggers, who had seen Pip with Estella, clearly notices the supposition which Pip takes no pains to hide. Later the housekeeper reappears twice, thus making Pip even more sure that his "conviction was the truth."

All in all, it is a dull evening; Wemmick is all business in his Little Britain personality. They leave, and after having gone a short distance, Wemmick assumes his Walworth sentiments and suggests that he too found the evening with Jaggers difficult. After sharing a few pleasantries, Pip asks Wemmick how Jaggers tamed Molly. Wemmick tells what he knows: twenty years ago Molly was quite handsome, was thought to have some gypsy blood in her, and was tried for murder and acquitted. Jaggers was her lawyer. His success in the case "may almost be said to have made him." The murder victim was a woman ten years older than the accused; she was also very much larger and stronger. Both had led tramping lives, but the younger (Molly) was married and known for her terrible temper. The vicious murder had taken place in a barn after a terrible struggle. Though there was no reason to suspect anyone but Molly, Jaggers pleaded her innocent and rested his case "on the improbabilities of her having been able to do it." At the same time, the prosecution attempted to prove that the jealous Molly had a young child. Jaggers simply refused to concern himself with that matter (since it could not be proved). Immediately after her acquittal, Molly went into Jaggers' service, tamed as she is now. The child was never again heard of, though it was said to have been a girl. Pip goes home to think over these new considerations.

Commentary

This chapter carefully traces two ironies. First, Estella's coldness and lack of passion are subtly contrasted with the passionate jealousy of her mother. Just as Estella had been taken over by Miss Havisham, so Molly had been taken over by Jaggers. In the latter case, Jaggers had not attempted to destroy in Molly the capacity to feel; rather he had tamed her by channeling her jealous passions toward more constructive ends. That she can still feel sympathy is demonstrated by her reactions to Jaggers' conversation with Pip concerning Estella's marriage to Drummle. The second irony adds a mood of pathos to Pip's situation. Since having first met Estella and witnessing her pride and haughtiness, Pip has consistently rejected elements of his social background because he feels they fall so far short of her. Now Pip must confront the fact that Estella's heritage is actually far more tainted than his.

CHAPTER 49

Summary

Pip goes to Satis House. There he finds Miss Havisham in the wedding feast room "sitting on the hearth in a ragged chair, close before, and lost in the contemplation of, the ashy fire." There is an "air of utter loneliness upon her" and Pip feels pity despite the wrongs she had wilfully dealt him in the past. Finally she looks up and asks: "Is it real?" When he assures her that it is he, Pip hears her solemn thanks and notes a new expression on her face, as if she were afraid of him. Miss Havisham, though she fears he can never believe it, wants to prove to him that she is not all stone. After reassuring her, Pip follows her request and explains the secret history of Herbert's partnership; he adds that he is now unable to continue financial contributions to the arrangement and requests that she do so. Miss Havisham agrees to contributing the necessary nine hundred pounds if Pip will keep her part in the situation secret just as he has kept his own. When Miss Havisham then asks if Pip is "very unhappy now," he cannot reply at the moment for his voice fails; then he suggests that there are also other secret causes for his unhappiness. She regrets the fact that she can only serve him by helping Herbert, but he answers her that this is quite enough. Miss Havisham provides Pip with a note to Jaggers which both authorizes payment of the money and assures her lawyer that Pip himself is not profiting from the transaction.

With trembling hands, she gives Pip her pencil without looking at him. She says that her name is written on the paper and — if he can ever find himself inclined to do so — she wants him to write beneath it the words "I forgive her." Pip answers: "I can do it now. There have been sore mistakes; and my life has been a blind and thankless one; and I want forgiveness and direction far too much, to be bitter with you." To Pip's amazement and terror, the repentant woman drops to her knees at his feet and raises her hands as if praying. Crying for the first time in Pip's presence, she will not be comforted and refuses to rise as she clings to his hand and sobs: "What have I done! What have I done!" Pip has no reply; he knows she has committed hideous acts and harbored evil desires, but he knows equally well that

> . . . in seclusion, she had secluded herself from a thousand natural and healing influences; that her mind, brooding solitary, had grown diseased, as all minds do and must and will that reverse the appointed order of their Maker.

Compassion alone fills him as he watches the woman punish herself and hears her say that she sees in his face a mirror of the pain which she once felt. Pip pleads with her to dismiss him from her mind and conscience. He suggests, rather, that she try to restore in Estella any part of that nature which was hidden from her by her training. Miss Havisham answers that when Estella first came to her she meant only to save her from the kind of misery she had experienced herself; then she adds:

> But as she grew, and promised to be very beautiful, I gradually did worse, and with my praises, and with my jewels, and with my teachings, and with this figure of myself always before her, a warning to back and point my lessons, I stole her heart away and put ice in its place.

Pip tells her sadly that he knows the history of her personal hurt, and he requests that she tell him of Estella's origins. She answers that she does not know the identity of the parents but that Jaggers brought her to Satis House when she was two or three; Estella herself knows nothing but that she was left an orphan. Pip is now thoroughly convinced of his earlier supposition concerning Molly.

Twilight is closing in as he takes his leave of the old woman. He goes downstairs and, since he senses he will never again return to the place, decides to walk around the old grounds one last time. Memories crowd his mind as he walks the paths he had walked on visits long past. In the old brewery the fanciful impression which appeared to him on his first visit recurs: he sees Miss Havisham hanging on the beam. The illusion causes him to shudder, and its seeming reality leads him to return to see if Miss Havisham is as safe and well as he had left her. Returning and looking into the room, he sees her still sitting near the fire with her back toward him. He begins to leave; suddenly he views a horrifying sight:

> I saw a great flaming light spring up. In the same moment I
> saw her running at me, shrieking, with a whirl of fire blazing
> all about her, and soaring at least as many feet above her head
> as she was high.

Pip throws his coat over her, drags the old tablecloth from the table (letting all the rottenness and ugly things of the feast preparation fall to the floor), and wrestles with her as if they were "desperate enemies." By the time Pip gathers his senses, Miss Havisham's wedding dress is a charred ruin, disturbed beetles and spiders are running about the floor, and the servants are gathering. Miss Havisham, though seriously burned, is in danger principally from nervous shock. Her bed is placed on the long table, where she can be treated, and she is dressed in white cotton-wool. Her last request before Pip leaves is that he write a statement of forgiveness; he does so, kisses her goodbye, and leaves for London — never to see Miss Havisham again.

CHAPTER 50

Summary

Pip's left arm is severely burned to the elbow and must be carried in a sling. Herbert, after returning from Hammersmith where he related the details of the accident to his family, goes to the chamber and spends the day tending to Pip's injuries. For Pip sleep is difficult; dreams of the glare of the flames, the fierce burning smell, and the sounds of Miss Havisham's shrieks recur. Herbert tells Pip that all is well with Magwitch. Last evening the fugitive had grown very talkative and had told Herbert much about his life. Among other things, he had told of breaking off a romance with a young, jealous, and revengeful woman. As Herbert relates the details of the romantic entanglement, Pip is quite moved and excited, especially when he is told that the woman was tried for murder, that she swore to Magwitch that she would kill their child, and that (though Jaggers defended her successfully) both she and the child disappeared after the trial. When Magwitch had seen Pip on the marshes long ago, he had been particularly moved because his own child (a girl whose whereabouts he no longer knew) would have been the same age. An excited Pip says to Herbert: "I know I am quite myself. And the man we have in hiding down the river, is Estella's Father."

CHAPTER 51

Summary

Pip is not himself sure what purpose he had in view when he was so "hot on tracing out and proving Estella's parentage." With "feverish conviction," he decides to see Jaggers "and come at the bare truth," though he does not know whether he does so for Estella's sake or "to transfer to the man in whose preservation |he| was so much concerned, some rays of the romantic interest that had so long surrounded her." Early the next morning, Pip goes to Jaggers' office and finds the lawyer and Wemmick together. Because of his bandaged arms and general appearance, Pip has first to explain the accident; then he produces the note which gives him Miss Havisham's authority to receive the nine hundred pounds for Herbert. Jaggers regrets the fact that money is not being paid to Pip himself, and both he and Wemmick show disapproval when Pip lets it be known that he had refused an offer from Miss Havisham which would have brought him "portable property." Pip then tells Jaggers that he requested from the old woman information about her adopted daughter. He adds that he has seen Estella's mother recently, though not so recently as Jaggers, and then for the first time gets the better of Jaggers in conversation: the lawyer is "brought to an indefinably attentive stop" when Pip says he also knows the identity of Estella's father. Jaggers does not himself know this; he moves noticeably when Pip says: "His name is Provis — from New South Wales." Jaggers asks Pip on what evidence Provis makes his claim. He is visibly startled by Pip's unexpected reply that Provis makes no such claim and does not, in fact, have any knowledge or belief that his daughter is alive. Then Pip tells all he knows, only leaving Jaggers to assume he received from Miss Havisham the information he had actually received from Wemmick. Jaggers attempts to leave the subject and go back to business; Pip, however, makes "a passionate, almost an indignant appeal" for the lawyer to be more frank and manly with him.

He states that he has been frank with Jaggers and that his love and concern for Estella make him deserve the truth. When Jaggers remains firm, Pip turns to Wemmick and refers to his Walworth life, to his old father, and to "all the innocent cheerful playful ways" with which he refreshes his business life. He begs Wemmick to help motivate Jaggers to be more candid on the subject of Estella.

At this statement, Wemmick and Jaggers look oddly at one another; then Jaggers relaxes into something like a smile and Wemmick becomes bolder. Jaggers, referring to what Pip has told him about Wemmick's life, says his assistant "must be the most cunning impostor in all London." Wemmick answers that he believes Jaggers also to be an impostor, then adds: "I shouldn't wonder if *you* might be planning and contriving to have a pleasant home of your own, one of these days, when you're tired of all this work." Jaggers nods his head in agreement, says the subject of "poor dreams" can be dropped since Pip knows more about them than he, and gives in to Pip's pleas, saying that (while he will admit nothing) he will relate a hypothetical case of interest to Pip. The case is as follows: A certain lawyer lives in an atmosphere of evil; all around he sees children being born in great numbers for certain destruction. Now, suppose a woman (in the circumstances Pip had mentioned) comes to a lawyer with a small child. This same lawyer also holds a position of trust with a rich and eccentric lady who wants to adopt and raise a child. Suppose that the child is pretty and can be one saved from the heap of the lost and that the father believes the child dead. Suppose the lawyer refuses to defend the woman unless she turns over the child to him; then, after successfully defending her, he decides to take her in and tame her passions. Then suppose years later the father, mother, and child are living in the same city. If one found these events to be facts, what would it gain one to make the information public? The child would certainly be dragged down in scandal and disgrace. Both Pip and Wemmick, after hearing Jaggers, swear secrecy.

After this, Wemmick and Jaggers go back to work. Pip notes that they seem suspicious, each conscious "of having shown himself in a weak and unprofessional light to the other." For this reason, they become uneasy. Both are relieved when a client comes and sheds a tear because of his situation. Practically in unison they say that no feeling is permitted in the office and that the client (Mike) must leave. With this act, they appear to have re-established their good understanding.

Commentary

Here Pip continues to redeem himself. By stating to Jaggers his refusal to make money from his relationship with Miss Havisham, he demonstrates an indifference to "respectable" wealth which would have — unlike Magwitch's fortune — given him social prestige. By agreeing that Estella's heritage should not be revealed, he demonstrates that this kind of defensive revenge which led him to write Trabb concerning his employee's behavior is no longer a part of his character. Pip accepts himself for what he is; he sees in the two-sided characters of both Jaggers and Wemmick that emotion is not universally a sign of weakness. By failing to aspire to wealth, by bearing social hurts with humility and by not resorting to revenge, by accepting the validity of true emotion, Pip clearly now symbolizes the virtues of his own heritage, the virtues symbolized throughout the novel by Joe, Biddy, and the world of the forge.

CHAPTER 52

Summary

Leaving Little Britain, Pip takes the check and immediately concludes with Clarriker the business concerning Herbert's expectations. In his new partnership capacity, Herbert will establish a branch office of the firm in the East; thus Pip sees that he must prepare himself for separation from his friend, a dread which is quickly overcome when Herbert arrives full of enthusiasm about the proceedings. Pip's burns suffered in the accident heal slowly. On a Monday morning in March he receives from Wemmick a note suggesting that the present week is suitable to attempt Magwitch's escape. It is decided, because the burns partially disable Pip, to request that Startop aid in the rowing, though he need know little of the project in which he is assisting. The destination is irrelevant to Pip; he has decided to accompany Magwitch wherever a steamer may take them. Pip, who will steer the boat, obtains passports; Startop agrees to provide his services; and Herbert passes on to Magwitch plans for the Wednesday which involve his (Magwitch's) coming down to the river on first signs of their boat. When Pip returns to the Temple on Monday afternoon, he finds in his box a dirty though not badly-written letter; it requests that he, if not afraid, come alone to the sluice-house in the marshes at nine in the evening on Monday or Tuesday, there to receive "information regarding *your uncle Provis.*" Since Tuesday night would be too close to the time of the planned escape, he must board a coach in half an hour to carry out the meeting on the present day. Leaving Herbert an ambiguous note, he arrives at his destination with just enough time to check on Miss Havisham's condition before setting out for the marshes. At the inn, he hears again the false story of Pumblechook's great contribution to his career, but he spends most of the available time thinking of his own ingratitude to the noble Joe.

CHAPTER 53

Summary

On the marshes it is a dark and windy night. Pip hesitates, half inclined to go back. After a ghostly half-hour walk, he approaches the desolate and abandoned sluice-house. Neither his knocking nor a call brings any response. Having entered the unlatched door and taken up a candle, he is immediately attacked, his candle extinguished, and a strong noose thrown over his neck from behind. A muffled voice says: "Now, I've got you." In moments his arms are pulled close to his sides, this causing great pain, and a strong man's chest deadens his shouts by pressing against his mouth. Faint with pain, he is in utter darkness until the man puts on a light; the man is Orlick, whom Pip had not expected and who now has him "in a dangerous strait indeed." Orlick calls Pip his enemy and reveals his intention: "I mean to do it all myself. One keeps a secret better than two." He accuses Pip of costing him his job at Miss Havisham's, of giving him a bad name and standing in his way with Biddy, and of saying that he would do anything to get him out of the country. Bringing down his fist viciously on the table, Orlick says: "I'm a-going to have your life!" He also accuses Pip of having always stood in his way. Now that will end: "I'll put your body in the kiln . . . and, let people suppose what they may of you, they shall never know nothing."

Rapidly Pip imagines what various people will make of his unexpected disappearance: Magwitch will believe himself deserted; Herbert will doubt him; Joe and Biddy will never be aware of the shame he feels for his previous behavior. Though the prospect of death is terrible, Pip finds "the dread of being misremembered after death" even more so. Half drunk, Orlick wishes to torment him before the murder; thus Pip resolves to "die making some last poor resistance to him." Orlick admits the attack on Mrs. Joe; he had left her for dead. However, Orlick claims, Pip was the actual attacker. While he was bullied and beaten, Pip was favored; this led Orlick to commit the act. Vivid images recur to Pip as he confronts his situation. He knows that Orlick is drinking to work himself into a state to commit the murder. Drinking more, Orlick tells of his now being in service to Compeyson and thus finding the facts of the Pip-Magwitch relationship. He tells Pip that he was the man at the foot of his stairs on the night of Magwitch's arrival. He warns that Magwitch is in just as desperate a circumstance as is Pip. As Orlick moves drunkenly and menacingly, Pip no longer has any hope left. Suddenly, he sees his attacker throw the bottle away and (swearing heavily) pick up a stone-hammer with a long heavy handle. Pip makes one last struggle and shouts with all his might.

Instantly he hears responsive shouts and soon sees Orlick being overcome by several men. After a brief period of unconsciousness, he views his rescuers: Trabb's boy, Herbert, and Startop. Orlick has fled. The rescuers assist in making Pip's arm less painful, and they all go to town together. The reason for Pip's good fortune is that, when leaving the Temple, he carelessly dropped the note from Orlick. Herbert and Startop were alarmed on finding it, and they immediately set out in pursuit. Since there was no word of him at Miss Havisham's, they had gone to the Blue Boar; there they found Trabb's boy ("true to his ancient habit of happening to be everywhere where he had no business") and he had led them into the marshes and to the sluice-house. Since they felt Pip might actually be gaining information about Magwitch, they had not entered immediately, but had waited until they heard his shout. To Trabb's boy they make light of the matter and pay him two guineas. They take the small carriage back to London. Pip becomes more and more ill. He spends most of Tuesday in bed, fearing at times that he is delirious and knowing that both his arm and head ache terrifically. At night he sleeps well, and on Wednesday he awakes feeling better and more able to carry out the escape.

CHAPTER 54

Summary
His mind wholly set on his benefactor's safety, Pip packs a few of his possessions and sets out for his unknown destination. The plan is to go down river after the ride, to spend the night below Gravesend in a public house, and the next day to flag down either the steamer for Rotterdam or the one for Hamburg. Pip, Herbert, and Startop pass the steamers, one of which they will stop next day, and soon arrive at Mill Pond Bank, where Magwitch first signals that all is well, and then walks down to the river's edge. As the boat moves back into the open river, Magwitch puts his arms around Pip and expresses thanks for his faithfulness. All of Magwitch's thoughts are centered on Pip's being set up as a great gentleman in a foreign country; Pip, however, is more concerned about the dangers of the moment and constantly looks for any suspicious occurrence. After rowing into the dismal evening, they finally spot a rather dirty but satisfactory place to get meals and lodging. During the time just before docking the boat, all have the feeling that they are being watched; thus Pip is quite attentive when a man at the public house who wears clothes taken from a drowned seaman washed ashore asks if they "had seen a four-oared galley going up with the tide." The boat carried two passengers whom the man thought to be custom officers. All of them (Pip especially) are made uneasy by this information: "A four-oared galley hovering about in so unusual a way as to attract this notice, was an ugly circumstance that |Pip| could not get rid of."

After Magwitch is sent to bed, Pip and his two comrades go outside and hold a meeting. They decide not to leave early in the morning and go downstream to await the steamer's afternoon arrival; rather, they will stay where they are "until within an hour or so of the steamer's time, and then . . . get out in her track, and drift easily with the tide." Pip goes to bed and awakes quite early. Looking out the window, he sees two men who first look at his boat, then head out across the marsh. At breakfast he relates what he has seen, but Magwitch (as usual) is the least nervous of the group and believes the men very likely belong to the Custom House. Nevertheless, Pip suggests the need for caution: he and Magwitch will walk away to a distant point where they can see and will let the boat take them aboard there (or as near there as possible) at about noon. Still Magwitch is unimpressed by any danger; he reassures Pip, though he also follows whatever cautions are suggested. The time comes for them to board the boat; they do so and row out into the track of the steamer. Finally (at half past one) smoke from both the steamers appears. Pip and Magwitch get their bags together and say an emotional goodbye to Herbert and Startop. Suddenly, the four-oared galley shoots out from under a bank and moves ahead of them in the steamer's path. Of the two sitters in the galley, one holds the rudder and looks at them attentively; the other is wrapped up much as Magwitch is, and he appears to shrink and to whisper some instructions to the steerer. Not a word is spoken in either boat. As the steamer for Hamburg approaches closely, the galley signals to Pip's boat. The steerer, just before running the galley near them, shouts:

You have a returned transport there . . . That's the man, wrapped in the cloak. His name is Abel Magwitch, otherwise Provis. I apprehend that man, and call upon him to surrender, and you to assist.

There is great confusion on the steamer as its passengers see the two small boats locked together. Pip hears the orders given to stop the steamer's paddles, but he also "felt her driving down upon us irresistibly." He sees the galley's steersman put a hand on Magwitch's shoulder, then sees his benefactor "start up, lean across his captor, and pull the cloak from the neck of the shrinking sitter in the galley": it is Compeyson, the convict whose face Pip recognizes from long ago on the marshes. The white terror on Compeyson's face is unforgettable. Then a great cry from the steamer is heard as it approaches Pip's boat.

The next thing Pip knows he is taken on board the galley. Herbert and Startop are there, but the two convicts have disappeared. The steersman keeps the boat straight. Just before the steamers pass, taking with them all hope of escape, Magwitch is seen injured and swimming nearby. All is lost: he is "taken on board, and instantly manacled at the wrists and ankles." Returning to the public house from which they had left, Pip is able to give Magwitch some comfort for his severe chest injury and deep head cut. Magwitch, despite the great pain caused by breathing, relates to Pip a story soon verified by the capturing officer: he had unmasked Compeyson; the villain had staggered back and pulled both of them overboard. The struggle had caused Pip's boat to capsize; then the two enemies "had gone down, fiercely locked in each other's arms, and . . . there had been a struggle under water, and [Magwitch] had disengaged himself, struck out, and swam away." Magwitch's injuries came from his having been struck by both the steamer and the galley. Though the arresting officer takes possession of all the prisoner's belongings (including his pocket book), he gives Pip permission both to provide Magwitch with dry clothes and to accompany him to London. The man at the public house who had dressed himself in the clothes of a drowned seaman is told where he may find Compeyson's body. Pip now feels his place is with Magwitch as long as he lives; all disgust for him has melted away:

> In the hunted, wounded, shackled creature who held my hand in his, I only saw a man who had meant to be my benefactor, and who had felt affectionately, gratefully, and generously, towards me with great constancy through a series of years. I only saw in him a much better man than I had been to Joe.

Because he knows Magwitch has no chance to avoid hanging, Pip cannot regret the fact that his injury is apparently fatal. He does everything to comfort the dying man: when Magwitch says he is content to have seen the boy and that he can now be a gentleman without him, Pip carefully avoids letting him know that under his circumstances the state confiscates all property held by the criminal. Then, when Magwitch also says Pip should (as a gentleman) stay away and not be seen with a common criminal, Pip replies: "I will never stir from your side, when I am suffered to be near you. Please God, I will be as true to you as you have been to me!" At this the convict's hand trembles and the old sob again is heard from his throat. Pip vows to himself "that he need never know how his hopes of enriching me had perished."

Commentary

Since the appearance of Compeyson at Wopsle's performance and the revelation of his intent by Orlick at the sluice-house, the inevitability of Magwitch's capture has been suggested. The capture itself, since it signifies the end of any chance of his continuing to enrich Pip, is Magwitch's greatest sacrifice. He did not have to make himself vulnerable, but he chose to come to England; his return makes Pip's fall from the grace of the forge a fortunate one. By giving Pip wealth, he presented to the young apprentice a choice for which the virtues of the forge were willingly and quickly sacrificed; by giving Pip himself, he provides a constructive return to those virtues. Like Joe, Pip no longer is concerned about wealth and its privileges. His concerns become human: a sincere devotion to the man whose sacrifices for him have been so great. Pip's preparation for faith has been brief; his baptism in the Thames near the warring forces of benevolence and evil solidify it.

CHAPTER 55

Summary

Magwitch is taken to police court next day and would be tried immediately, but after Compeyson's death it is necessary to send for an officer from the old prison ship to have the convict identified. Pip goes to Jaggers and requests that he defend Magwitch. He also tells the lawyer that the fate of the convict's wealth must be kept a secret. Jaggers is angry that Pip has let a fortune slip through his fingers and suggests that some attempt be made to recover part; however, Pip is little interested and resolves he will "never be sickened with the hopeless task of attempting to establish |a claim|." When Compeyson's body is found (horribly disfigured and miles from the scene of his death), contents of his pockets indicate that, as the informer, he had, after obtaining accurate knowledge from New South Wales concerning Magwitch's wealth, hoped for a reward out of the convict's fortune. After three days' delay, the witness comes and identifies Magwitch; trial is set for one month later. At this trying time in Pip's life, Herbert brings news that he must leave immediately to set up his company's branch office in Cairo. Concerned about Pip's future (which is now completely uncertain), Herbert delicately offers him a position as a clerk in the branch office and suggests that he could live with him and Clara (though Clara is not yet going, since her duty lies with her father as long as he lives). Both Pip's concern for Magwitch and other considerations lead him to decline the offer for the present; he promises to make some final decision within three months.

Later in the week, Herbert leaves, and as Pip returns to his empty quarters he encounters Wemmick knocking at his door. "In his private and personal capacity," Wemmick explains the reason for his error in suggesting an appropriate time to attempt the escape:

> I kept my ears open, seeming to have them shut, until I heard that |Compeyson| was absent, and I thought that would be the best time for making the attempt. I can only suppose now, that it was a part of his policy, as a very clever man, habitually to deceive his own instruments.

Pip readily assures Wemmick that he does not consider him responsible; then, when Wemmick says he regrets "the sacrifice of so much portable property," Pip replies: "What *I* think of, Wemmick, is the poor owner of the property." Pip and Wemmick go upstairs for a drink, and Wemmick asks Pip to "oblige" by accompanying him on a walk between eight and twelve next Monday morning; it is to be Wemmick's first holiday in twelve years. Because Wemmick has done so much for him, Pip foregoes his desire to be alone and accepts the invitation.

On Monday Pip arrives punctually at the castle. Wemmick strikes him "as looking tighter than usual, and having a sleeker hat on." The walk proceeds and soon they approach a church; at the door, the Aged is escorting Miss Skiffins, and Wemmick suddenly says: "Let's have a wedding." After the clerk and clergyman arrive, the wedding proceeds, with Pip acting as best man. The ceremony concluded, they all go to breakfast at a pleasant little tavern. Pip wishes them well and before leaving is made to agree that the events of the morning (which have been carried out in Wemmick's Walworth sentiments) will not be mentioned in Little Britain. Jaggers might well think his assistant had suffered a softening of the brain.

CHAPTER 56

Summary

Two broken ribs had wounded one of Magwitch's lungs; thus, as he lies ill in prison, pain makes it impossible for him to speak much. Soon he is transferred to the infirmary (where Pip is allowed to be with him), and it becomes Pip's duty to read to him. From the day the prison door had closed on the unfortunate convict, he became weaker and worse; "the kind of submission or resignation that he showed, was that of a man who was tired out." Humble and regretful, he never complains or attempts to justify himself. His trustful look implies his belief that Pip has found some redeeming feature in him. The trial is short; he is found guilty. On the final day of the sessions — after the judge has made a highly rhetorical speech — Magwitch and thirty-one others are given the death sentence. Though Pip writes several letters to men in high authority, he soon realizes they will have no effect. None of the guards is hard with Magwitch or Pip, who visits him daily. Each day they assure Pip (as he hopes death will come naturally before the date of execution) that the prisoner's health is failing. Ten days later, Magwitch is noticeably worse. Pip (suffering in the remembrance that he had once meant to desert him) hears the convict say: "And what's the best of all, you've been more confortable alonger me, since I was under a dark cloud, than when the sun shone. That's best of all." The allotted time for Pip's visit ends but the warden (sensing that Magwitch is close to death) permits him to stay. Magwitch's last words are a response to Pip's inquiry about his pain: "I don't complain of none, dear boy." Momentarily the film clears from the dying man's eyes; at that moment (feeling the pressure of his hand) Pip tells him that the daughter whom he had loved and thought lost is alive, that she is a lady and very beautiful, and that he loves her. Magwitch raises Pip's hand to his lips, then dies quietly. Pip can find no better words for parting than these: "O Lord, be merciful to him, a sinner!"

CHAPTER 57

Summary

Left wholly alone, Pip gives notice of his intention to leave his apartment in the Temple as soon as he can legally do so; in the meantime he plans to sub-lease the quarters. As he accumulates his bills and realizes his lack of money, he begins to be seriously alarmed by the state of his affairs. But illness and fever now overcome him suddenly and prevent him from concentrating clearly on his financial affairs. For a day or so, he lies on the sofa; then "one night |comes| which appeared of great duration, and which teemed with anxiety and horror." Trying to sit up in bed next morning, he finds he cannot do so. Over a period of time dreadful hallucinations appear to him; some of these involve various tortures by those to whom he owes money. As this goes on, a tendency develops for the people near him to look like Joe. At last, he takes courage and asks: "*Is* it Joe?" The affirmative reply breaks his heart; he begs Joe to look angry at him, to strike him, to tell him of his ingratitude — anything but to be so good to him. Instead, Joe puts his head on the pillow at his side, places his arms around his neck, and expresses great joy that Pip is finally able to recognize him. Joe says: "You and me was ever friends. And when you're well enough to go out for a ride — what larks!" Pip, unable to get up and express his emotion, says simply: "O God bless this gentle Christian man!" From Joe Pip finds that his fever and illness have lasted almost two months; during that time, Joe (following Biddy's suggestion) has been with him practically every minute. Joe obviously takes pride in Biddy's having taught him to write; he sends a note to her telling of Pip's improved condition.

Then Joe relates other news to Pip: Miss Havisham died, leaving four thousand pounds to Matthew Pocket (largely because of what Pip had said of him) and practically all the rest of her fortune to Estella; Orlick broke into Pumblechook's house, and before being captured took the pretentious man's cash box, drank his wine, ate his food, slapped his face, pulled his nose, stuffed his mouth full of flowers, and tied him to a bedpost. As Pip slowly gains strength, he feels himself a child again being cared for by the tender protectiveness of Joe's hands. They both look forward to the day when they can ride together. Finally they are able to do so, and the "summer growth was already on the trees and on the grass, and sweet summer scents filled all the air." The beauty is too much for Pip. He puts his head on Joe's shoulder and thinks: "There was no change whatever in Joe. Exactly what he had been in my eyes [in childhood], he was in my eyes still; just as simply faithful, just as simply right." Pip feels that he should ask Joe if he knows the details about Magwitch; however, Joe's concern is for Pip, and he immediately suggests that they avoid topics "for ever onnecessary." As Pip becomes stronger and better, Joe becomes a little uneasy with him; he goes back to concluding his sentences with "Sir." This does not please Pip, but he knows he is to blame. He is ashamed to admit his actual poverty and debt for fear that Joe will try to help him financially.

On a Sunday they have a quiet and pleasant ride together. Pip has resolved that on Monday morning he will tell Joe that he has decided not to join Herbert, that his intention is to marry Biddy — these decisions will convince Joe that he will never again return to the pride of earlier days. That evening, Joe enters the room where Pip lies in bed. He asks if Pip is sure he is well, and when Pip assures him of this he pats the coverlet and in a noticeably husky voice says "Good-night." Pip arises next morning eager to carry out his resolution without delay. He hurries to the breakfast table. Joe is not there; he has left a letter which includes a receipt for the debt and costs on which Pip has been arrested. It also includes a note: "Not wishful to intrude I have departured fur you are well again dear Pip and will do better without Jo. P.S. Ever the best of friends." To this moment Pip had supposed that his creditors had withdrawn or suspended proceedings until his recovery; he had never dreamed of Joe's paying the money. Pip's plan is now clear: he will go to the forge and speak to Joe, then go to Biddy and humbly offer to mold his life in any way that will make him worthy to marry her.

CHAPTER 58

Summary

News of the heavy fall of Pip's high fortunes reaches his native town before he does. He discovers that there is a new coolness toward him when he arrives at the Blue Boar. Though he is tired after the trip, he finds his old room no longer available and must settle for a quite inferior lodging. Next morning before breakfast he strolls to Satis House; there he finds that it has been sold for building materials and that all the furnishings are to be auctioned. He returns to the Blue Boar's dining room and finds Pumblechook waiting to have breakfast with him. The haughty gentleman says with a magnificently forgiving yet derogatory air: "Young man, I am sorry to see you brought low. But what else could be expected!" Frowning, yet too weak to quarrel, Pip sits down at the table. Finally having taken as much of his uncle's smug forgiveness as he can stand, Pip suggests that he be left alone. With this opportunity, Pumblechook refers to his own part in achieving Pip's former position. Pip is aware that the landlord and waiter (not he) are the intended audience, but he continues to listen as Pumblechook makes numerous claims to kindness delivered in the boy's youth.

After this ordeal, "it was only the pleasanter to turn to Biddy and to Joe, whose great forbearance shone more brightly than before if that could be, contrasted with this brazen pretender." They will never, as Pumblechook has just done, suggest that Pip's state is the reward ingratitude deserves. His heart softened as he returns toward the forge, Pip hopes to see Biddy at the schoolhouse where she is mistress. However, neither it nor Biddy's house is occupied. He goes on toward the forge, listening for the sound of Joe's hammer; but he soon notes that the forge too is closed. "But, the house was not deserted, and the best parlour seemed to be in use, for there were white curtains fluttering in its window, and the window was open and gay with flowers." As Pip enters, Biddy (arm in arm with Joe) gives a cry and runs to embrace him. Both weep; then Biddy explains: "It's my wedding-day, and I am married to Joe." Their day now made complete, Joe and Biddy are overjoyed by Pip's presence. Pip's first thought is one of thankfulness that he never mentioned his own hopes to Joe; then he warmly congratulates both of them, thanks them for the charitable acts with which they have repaid his own ingratitude, and says that he is going abroad to work — there to earn money to repay Joe (though, he knows, the debt can never be canceled). Pip expresses his hope that when they have a son of their own, they will not tell him that the boy who lived here before was so ungrateful, but that he has grown into a man who honors them both. Their hearts melt as the humbled Pip requests forgiveness. He goes to London, sells all his belongings, and within two months joins Herbert as a clerk in Clarriker and Co. Within four months Pip assumes individual responsibility of the eastern branch while Herbert returns to London to marry Clara, whose father has recently died. Many years pass before Pip becomes a partner in the firm, and during the period he lives happily with Herbert and Clara, pays his debts, lives sparingly, and maintains a correspondence with Joe and Biddy. Finally, when he becomes a partner in the firm, Clarriker's conscience demands that he tell of Pip's part in Herbert's success. Herbert is moved and amazed, and Pip decides that the incompetence he had thought was Herbert's had actually been his own. The business is not a great one, but by working hard they achieve a good name and do well enough. Finally Pip is entirely comfortable.

CHAPTER 59

Summary

For eleven years Pip has not seen Joe or Biddy. One December evening an hour or two after dark, he places his hand on the latch of the old kitchen door. Unseen, he views Joe "smoking his pipe in the old place by the kitchen firelight, as healthy and strong as ever, though a little grey." Near Joe, sitting on Pip's little stool, is a boy who to Pip appears to be himself. Joe, delighted by Pip's appearance, says: "We giv' him the name of Pip for your sake, dear old chap, and we hoped he might grow a little bit like you, and we think he do." Pip takes his namesake for a walk down by the cemetery where he had first met Magwitch. They understand each other "to perfection." After dinner, he tells Biddy that she must lend him the boy one day. She replies that he should marry, a suggestion which he considers unlikely. Biddy asks if he still suffers for Estella. He responds that, like all the foremost events of his life, he has not forgotten her: "But that poor dream, as I once used to call it, has all gone by, Biddy, all gone by!"

There are two endings to *Great Expectations*. The following summary provides first the original, then the revised ending:

FIRST ENDING: Two more years pass before Pip sees Estella. During this period, he hears of her leading an unhappy life, of her being separated from her cruel husband ("who had become quite renowned as a compound of pride, brutality, and meanness"), of the accidental death of her husband, caused by his beating a horse, "and of her being married again to a Shropshire doctor, who, against his interest, had once very manfully interposed" on the occasion of one of Drummle's brutal treatments of Estella. Pip is in London walking with young Pip when a servant comes running after him and asks him to step back and speak to a lady in a carriage. It is Estella, and they look very sadly at each other; she shakes his hand and kisses the child. Pip later is glad to have had the interview,

> . . . for, in her face and in her voice, and in her touch, she gave |him| the assurance that suffering had been stronger than Miss Havisham's teaching, and had given her a heart to understand what |his| heart used to be.

REVISED ENDING: For Estella's sake, Pip goes alone that evening to visit the site of Satis House. He has heard of Estella's unhappy life and also of the pride, greed, brutality, and meanness that had characterized her husband before his accidental death as the result of mistreating a horse. He looks at the empty lot which has nothing left but the wall of the old garden; then, looking along the desolate garden walk, he suddenly sees a solitary figure who shows itself aware of his presence. Though greatly changed, it is Estella. The freshness of her beauty is gone, "but its indescribable majesty and its indescribable charm remained." Besides these, there are characteristics which Pip has never before sensed in her: "the saddened softened light of the once proud eyes" and "the friendly touch of the once insensible hand."

86

They sit on a bench. For both it is the first visit to the old site. The ground is now Estella's only possession; it alone symbolizes the determined resistance she made in all the years in which everything else was sacrificed. They discuss Pip's business position, their old relationship, and their last parting. Estella says: "Suffering has been stronger than all other teaching, and has taught me to understand what your heart used to be. I have been bent and broken, but — I hope — into a better shape." Pip takes her hand and they walk from the ruined place. He sees "no shadow of another parting from her."

SUMMARY OF IMPORTANT DEVELOPMENTS

1. The chief problem confronting Pip becomes the protection of Magwitch from the law. By his loving care, Pip comforts Magwitch until the man's death.

2. Pip learns the details of the convict's story.

3. Pip is told the details of Miss Havisham's tragedy, which is brought to a close in this section.

4. Estella's wretched marriage to Drummle takes place, and his death occurs.

5. Herbert marries Clara after her father's death; Wemmick marries Miss Skiffins; and Joe marries Biddy.

6. Pip arranges to establish Herbert as a partner in a shipping firm, and persuades Miss Havisham to be generous to her young relative.

7. Thanks to Pip, Mr. Matthew Pocket receives a legacy from Miss Havisham.

8. Pip discovers Magwitch and Mr. Jaggers' housekeeper, Molly, to be the parents of Estella.

9. Orlick's attempted murder of Pip leads to his confession of having given Mrs. Joe her fatal injury. When last heard of, he is in the county jail after breaking into Pumblechook's house.

10. The death of Compeyson, who ruined Miss Havisham's life, is brought about by Magwitch in a struggle when the former betrays Magwitch.

11. A true reconciliation is effected by Pip when he apologizes to Joe and Biddy for his long neglect during his prosperity.

12. When Pip, after eleven years in the east, returns to England, he meets Estella at Satis House. She, like him, has been disciplined by life, and made a worthier person. Pip now sees in the moonlight "no shadow of another parting from her."

Structure

Methods of Analyzing Structure

The term "structure," when applied to narrative, denotes the element or elements which ideally provide unity for the story line. The term "plot," as opposed to "story," implies that a work has a certain structure (based on cause and effect), for "plot" denotes a series of actions each motivated by a single preceding action or by some combination of the preceding actions. As E. M. Forster says, plot is "a narrative of events, the emphasis falling on causality." If the reader wishes to discuss the structure of a novel, then, his problem is to isolate and evaluate the ways by which the novelist in question connects the various actions which constitute his plot. Before one can explain the effect and relevancy of plot connection, he must take careful note of the order of events.

1. Analysis

At the beginning of every novel, the protagonist (i.e., central character) exists in some state. He is of a particular age, race, sex, moral character; and he both lives in an environment which is usually described thoroughly and possesses a heritage which is of consequence to the way in which he acts. Plot begins when the state of the protagonist is altered — either with or without his knowledge. The alteration may be merely one of circumstance; this the reader may detect most easily. On the other hand, it may be one of values, of morals, of knowledge, or of a subtle combination of these. From this point to the end of the novel, a series of such alterations takes place.

After thorough recognition of the sequence of events, one must proceed to analyze, first, the reasons things happen (causality) and, second, the reason they happen in the order presented. In a well-written novel, events and the character of the protagonist come together, and their mutual effect alters the protagonist's response to subsequent events and circumstances. It is not enough, then, simply to ask if a given action is plausible in terms of the logic of the original character delineation; the reader must also ask whether it is plausible after the character has changed.

2. Foreshadowing and Juxtaposition

A novelist seldom presents a major reversal or climax in plot without preparing for it in some way. Likewise, he seldom presents major scenes of either parallel or corresponding significance without demonstrating through imagery, language, or similarity in plot that relationships exist which merit examination.

As in the analysis of plot, the reader who wishes to note an author's use of foreshadowing and juxtaposition should begin by paying careful attention to any aspect of the novel which recurs; then he should attempt to explain the effects of such recurrence. The recurring element may be a plot situation which on first appearance shows the protagonist in conflict with a minor force. Then the situation recurs with the protagonist pitted against the novel's major antagonist. In Melville's *Billy Budd,* for example, there is an allusion to a fight between Billy and a seaman named Red Whiskers, the cause of which is Billy's inability to speak in defense of himself. That scene clearly foreshadows the blow which Billy — unable to speak in his own defense — deals the antagonist Claggart at the climax of the novel. The scenes are not patterned; that is, they are not of parallel or corresponding significance; but the first does prepare the reader for (foreshadow) the second. In *The Scarlet Letter,* on the other hand, there are three scaffold scenes: one appears at the beginning of the novel, one in the middle, and one at the end. The similar emphasis which Hawthorne devotes to each demands that the reader explore the possibility of mutual relationships.

3. Emphatic Unity and Episode

In Greek tragedy the "episode" was a segment of action set between two choral songs. This idea of episode, denoting a completed incident, was very much a part of the early English novel. Eighteenth-century novels quite often include episodes which do nothing to further plot development; they often are merely anecdotes, essays, or brief tales which the author includes in his work to vary the kind of entertainment offered by the novel's plot. The reader today, schooled by more modern novels, usually does not appreciate this loose episodic structure and declares that it damages moods of intensity; he may also, since modern readers are noticeably practical, declare that the episodes are simply irrelevant.

The nineteenth and twentieth centuries saw an emphasis on unity. The novelist devoted himself to constructing a "well-made novel" in which irrelevancies were eliminated, tonal intensity emphasized, and intrusions of authorial commentary minimized (though this last did not gain general acceptance until the late nineteenth century). This tight structure necessarily focuses the reader's attention; it also requires him to evaluate the relevance of episodes which at first glance may appear irrelevant.

4. Scene and Summary

A now classic distinction employed by modern critics concerns the nature of the novelist's various methods of plot revelation. Some actions are summarized; that is, the author in different degrees of thoroughness tells *about* the actions. Other actions are *presented*: background and details are thoroughly drawn; dialogue is often employed heavily; entrances, exits, and movements of characters are carefully depicted. The scenic mode demands careful reader attention and tends to emphasize the action; the summary mode tends to de-emphasize the situation or to offer a method of foreshortening time and scene changes. In *The Structure of Literature,* Paul Goodman states that the scenic method absorbs the audience as if they are viewing the actual world: "This effect can be achieved by the permanence of place and the continuity of time; without such permanence and continuity, there is the introduction of the narrator's arrangements, and identification with the nonspatial narrating."

Having noted the nature of plot revelation by distinguishing between scene and summary, the reader should both notice scenes which may have relevance beyond their contribution to narrative progression and should observe the methods by which scenes are connected. In the former instance, the "tableau" is the scenic technique most often used. A tableau is a scene in which the position or positions of a silent and motionless person or group merges with physical surroundings so as to reflect graphically emotional, psychological, or moral relationships.

Scenes are most often connected by one of the following relationships: *chronological* (sequence in time); *expository* (as a narrator may recount or present in succession scenes which solidify an argument); and *spatial* (as images and scenes occur to the conscious or unconscious mind of the narrator). As a subcategory of spatial relationship, the *montage* is quite often used to connect scenes presented in the present with scenes or images which are recalled from the past. In this use, the term "montage" denotes a sequence of scenes produced by the narrator's associating an idea or mental image with its counterpart in a scene in the past. A conscious technical device which at times bears resemblance to the montage is the *segue,* a term more often applied to music and cinema. With respect to fiction, a segue functions by the writer's focusing on a fictional object, then withdrawing and presenting the same object in a difference scene and context.

Chart:
Guide to Main Action and Location
(Chapter References Appear in Parentheses Preceding Entry)

	Joe's house and forge	Satis House	Marshes
First Stage of Expectations (Chaps. 1-19)	(2) Pip steals food and file (7) Joe tells of his youth; later, news of Miss Havisham's invitation comes (9) Pip lies about visit to Satis House (15) Joe and Orlick fight; Mrs. Joe found after attack (19) Pip's departure for London	(8) Pip's first visit; insulted by Estella (11) Second visit; meets Pockets and Herbert (12) Pip becomes accustomed to Miss Havisham and wheeling her (13) Joe's visit to discuss Pip's indentures	(1) Pip's first meeting with Magwitch (3) Pip mistakenly approaches Compeyson and again meets Magwitch (5) Magwitch and Compeyson captured (17) Pip takes Biddy into his confidence
Second Stage of Expectations (Chaps. 20-39)	(35) Pip attends burial of Mrs. Joe	(29) Pip shocked by Estella's new elegance (38) Miss Havisham begs for Estella's love in Pip's presence	
Third Stage of Expectations (Chaps. 40-59)	(57) Pip's illness; Joe's caring for him; their reconciliation (58) Marriage of Joe and Biddy	(44) Miss Havisham expresses regret for her triumph (49) Miss Havisham requests Pip's forgiveness (59) Reunion of Pip with Estella	(53) Pip attacked by Orlick at sluice-house

Pip's home town	Jaggers' house and office	Pip's London dwellings	Other
(10) Stranger with file approaches Pip (18) Jaggers brings news of expectations			
(30) Pip comically deflated by Trabb's boy	(20) Pip observes Jaggers' clients (21) Pip meets Wemmick (26) Jaggers entertains Pip and his fellow students	(21) Pip disappointed by Barnard's Inn and recognizes Herbert (22) Herbert's monologue clarifies Miss Havisham-Estella relationship (27) Joe's uncomfortable visit (39) Magwitch's appearance at Temple	(23) Pip meets Matthew Pocket and Drummle (25) Pip visits Wemmick at Walworth (28) Pip overhears conversation of convicts in coach (31) Pip and Herbert attend Wopsle's *Hamlet* (32) Pip accompanies Wemmick to Newgate Prison (38) Pip arranges to help Herbert
(43) Pip confronts Drummle	(51) Pip tells Jaggers he knows Estella's parents	(40) Herbert meets Magwitch (42) Magwitch tells the story of his youth	(46) Pip recognizes a deepened feeling for Magwitch (47) Compeyson behind Pip at theater (52) Pip concludes business with Clarriker (54) Magwitch's unsuccessful escape attempt (55) Wemmick's marriage (56) Magwitch's death (58) Pip goes to work for Clarriker and Co.

Questions and Answers on Structure

Question 1.

Is Pip's ultimate acceptance and devotion to Magwitch believable in terms of his previous actions?

Answer

Pip's mind is consistently given to accepting absolute contrasts: to him Satis House is everything that Joe's home is not; Joe is the exact opposite of Magwitch; Drummle is everything Estella should not accept; Matthew is antithetical to all the other Pockets; Orlick is everything which renders him unsatisfactory for Biddy. Though Pip's observations may at times be correct, his tendency always to equate one pole with everything favorable and the other with everything unpleasant eventually leads him to be taken in by appearances.

Pip is born an orphan with no expectations. In this position he is most influenced by the virtuous Joe. Because he himself suffers indignities and persecution from all except the blacksmith, he appreciates the relief offered by Joe and is also able to identify sympathetically with the persecuted convict (Magwitch) whom he meets on the marshes. To help the convict, he steals — not so much from fear as from simple charity; that Joe later tells Magwitch he is welcome to the food he supposedly stole demonstrates that Pip had acted in the spirit of charity symbolized by Joe.

Pip's world is widened by the invitation to Miss Havisham's. Now, for the first time, he is furnished with other standards for contrast. By the time Jaggers appears to announce the expectations, Pip's tendency to see the world in terms of opposites has been well demonstrated: Estella is all Biddy is not; the crudity of Mrs. Joe and her circle is all that Satis House is not; Joe's clothes, speech, and simple pleasures are opposed to the apparent sophistication which characterizes the Satis House world.

When Magwitch reappears, Pip begins to question the accuracy of his previous value judgments. Though at first he feels only revulsion for the convict, he soon becomes aware of a maze of facts which alter his opinions so as to make his final devotion to Magwitch believable. First, he recognizes that Miss Havisham is not a fairy godmother; rather, she is a pitiable neurotic whose life and surroundings are rotting before her eyes. If anything, her treatment of her adopted daughter Estella has been far less benevolent than Pip's own treatment by Mrs. Joe — not to mention Joe himself. Moreover, he finds that Estella is the daughter of a murderess and a convict, his benefactor, Magwitch.

Pip's final acceptance of Magwitch is adequately motivated. Once he has no expectations, he no longer has the need for pretence. Like the boy who long ago felt pity for a stranger on the marshes, he can now feel more than pity; the convict is no longer a stranger, but a man who overcame a background of crime, made an honorable fortune abroad, and risked it all to return and make himself known to the one person who had ever felt compassion for him.

Question 2.

Does the structure of *Great Expectations* adequately prepare the reader for Pip's apparent winning of Estella at the end of the novel?

Answer

Dickens showed the manuscript of the novel to his eminent fellow novelist, Bulwer-Lytton, who advised Dickens to change the ending to make it "happy." That he was able to persuade Dickens to alter the original ending suggests at first glance that the author had again succumbed to his love for melodrama. Indeed, the probability of a chance meeting by two people in a desolate lot on the occasion of the initial return by both to a spot not visited in more than eleven years is unlikely, to say the least. Moreover, a meeting at dusk of a once proud woman who has been broken by harsh circumstances and a mature and moderately successful man who has remained devoted to her despite continual rejection for about twenty years is, certainly, open to suspicion of sentimentality. In spite of these facts, the final confrontation does not alter the tone of the novel. The structure prepares adequately for Pip's apparent winning of Estella.

Pip begins his pursuit of Estella by diminishing himself. In their first meeting she humiliates him by criticizing his origins; he reacts not by recognizing her for the cold snob she is (as Herbert had done), but accepts her judgment as true and denies any value in himself. Literally becoming without self, he cannot pursue her. Later Jaggers brings news of his expectations, but the ambiguity of their source hampers in two ways any potential pursuit of Estella: first, the pose he adopts is so shallow that it fails to compensate for the self he has denied. A vigorous pursuit of Estella is certainly impossible if he can fall victim to so unworthy an adversary as Trabb's boy. Second, Pip can see no real need for determined action; his belief that Miss Havisham is his benefactress leads him to rationalize every apparent failure in his relation to Estella, even her own warning that his desire is both useless and dangerous. Throughout most of the novel, Pip's pursuit is weak; it is never amorous. What he professes to be his love for Estella is in fact a grotesque self-sacrifice which contains no element of sexual desire. He has accepted, even before Miss Havisham offers it, her static definition of love:

> I'll tell you what real love is. It is blind devotion, unquestioning self-humiliation, utter submission, trust and belief against

94

yourself and against the whole world, giving up your whole heart and soul to the smiter.

Numerous events foreshadow Pip's initial failure in winning Estella. When Jaggers entertains Pip and his friends, he astutely describes Drummle's character as dangerous but at the same time a nature "of the true sort." Drummle is a spider; he has no intellect, but (as Pip himself later observes) he has the patience of his tribe and is willing to lie in wait and — without scruples — grasp what he wants. By the "true sort," Jaggers means that Drummle has no false front to weaken his force of character: he has no concern for people, for social amenities, for any concept of honor, or for anything but the gratification of his brute desires. Though Pip is not aware of Jaggers' implied comparison, he is of course the exact opposite of Drummle. Weakened by his delusions, he has no more hope of combating Drummle successfully than he had of combating Trabb's boy. Later, after both Pip and Jaggers know that Drummle has won Estella, Jaggers makes it clear that the result of the marriage is uncertain: without the possibility of dominating by intellect, Drummle must by his brute force "turn to and beat her" if he is to succeed in getting "the strength on his side." Pip can hardly make himself listen to Jaggers; he finds the possibility of brute force repulsive and is unwilling to accept the fact that a nature like Estella's can only be made submissive by such force.

A second significant patterned juxtaposition is revealed gradually in the novel. Pip and Estella are both orphans. Pip's essential humanity is easily, though temporarily, shaped by Joe, while Estella's wild charm — inherited from her murderess mother — is easily molded by Miss Havisham. Both Pip and Estella are either shaped into something outside their essential nature or adopt poses which disguise their nature. Pip is made an ingrate and a snob, Estella a heartless weapon to be used against all men; Magwitch and Miss Havisham, the respective sources of their expectations, both act as a result of indignities suffered at the hands of Compeyson. Their respective protégés, however, vary in insight. Estella, who calls Pip both "ridiculous" and a "visionary" boy, sees through Pip's facade though she does not recognize that beneath her coldness and hardness also lies a suppressed and different personaltiy. Pip, on the other hand, recognizes himself for the snob he is (as his recurrent pangs of conscience indicate); however, he cannot see beneath Estella's outward nature. In his mind she is beautiful beyond belief, rich, distant, hard, sophisticated, and born to the role she occupies.

Dickens prepares for Pip's final winning of Estella by concurrently depicting Pip's casting off of his façade and de-mythologizing Estella, and by alluding to Estella's nature being brought to the surface through her suffering at the hands of Drummle. The Estella Pip wins is not the goddess he considered her to be: the "freshness of her beauty" is gone; her property and expectations have vanished; she is revealed to be the daughter of a murderess and a convict. Pip no longer considers her an object to fill a social void in his own life; thus he can approach her affirmatively. Now the values of the forge are considered positive forces by Pip; he can offer them to her, but he will not negate himself by denying their existence.

Quetion 3.

Discuss the function of pictorial and dramatic devices in the opening scene of *Great Expectations*.

Answer

Unlike most of Dickens' novels, the opening scene of *Great Expectations* has little exposition. The reader is immediately introduced to the major themes, symbols, and the action which serves as a stimulus for most of the protagonist's reactions. The first-person narrator, a man who is recalling a youthful experience, maintains tension by narrating chronologically and by attempting to reveal as nearly as possible his childhood rather than his adult reactions to the experience.

Chapter 1 begins with a brief summary, then proceeds to a scene of dramatic intensity which casts doubt on Henry James' theory that no scene rendered by a first-person narrator can be dramatic. Dickens avoids the problem of the limitations of the protagonist's vision by making Pip, the mature narrator, view Pip, the youthful "small bundle of shivers," in much the same objective manner that a third-person Jamesian narrator views and recounts a protagonist's actions. In short order, the summary provides several necessary details: Pip is an orphan whose only awareness of his parents consists of fanciful impressions derived from the shape, size, and inscriptions on their tombstones. He is observant, imaginative, and a resident of the marsh country south of the Thames.

The narrator justifies the detail and precision of the scene he recounts by directly commenting that on that "memorable raw afternoon towards evening" he had received his "most vivid and broad impression of the identity of things." The "things" of which he becomes aware — his fears, in the presence of death, made prominent by his standing alone among weeds in a bleak marshland churchyard which holds the bodies of his parents and five brothers — provide a gothic atmosphere appropriate to the scene which follows.

A grotesquely embittered and suffering convict appears. His arising from among the graves is particularly dramatic, and the meeting with Pip is almost entirely by dialogue and interspersed descriptions of character movement. Initially, the dialogue is characterized by short questions and statements, each revealing the convict's impatient desires and needs and the boy's terror. Then the convict issues his demand for food and a file while the speechless Pip views him from atop a gravestone. After this, the convict issues his warning and leaves. Pip watches him carefully before running home with his mind filled with images of death and persecution. The vividness and terror of the metaphors that cross his mind at the close of the chapter contrast with the childish and whimsical thoughts that open it.

By combining a narrative, inside view with dramatic presentation, Dickens quite early in the novel reveals to the reader that Pip's imaginative mind is one in which fact, fancy, and atmosphere are at times confused. At the same time, the two tableau scenes — Pip's being physically turned upside down and the resultant distorted view of the world, and the convict's retreat against the background of the graves — foreshadow both recurring themes and strands of action in the novel. Of particular note are the following: (1) Pip becomes aware of isolation from family and of the desolation which surrounds him. Characteristically the Dickens hero is born without expectations; he achieves them or imagines them as a result of growing awareness of his actual deprivation. (2) The convict's turning Pip upside down causes the boy to have a distorted vision of the realities which surround him; likewise, later in the novel, Magwitch's benevolence causes the same distortion to take place. (3) To Pip's eyes, his shuddering body retreating through the gravestones and being attacked by nature in the form of briars, weeds, and cold appears to be eluding hands of the dead which beckon and grasp at it. Later, as the boy runs in fear, he notes that everything around the river is crooked and distorted except for two black and upright forms — one a beacon by which sailors steer and the other a post on which criminals are hanged and left exposed after execution. These and other images of persecution recur throughout the novel. (4) As Pip watches the convict go toward the hanging post, he is startled by the thought that the convict is like a pirate who has been hanged, returned to life and come down from the post, and now goes "back to hook himself up again." The criminal Magwitch, of course, enacts this foreshadowed sequence. Locked up in prison for his crimes, he later makes a new life for himself in New South Wales — only to return to England and almost certain death. Just as Pip the child is shocked by the idea, Pip the man is shocked by the reality. (5) The convict warns Pip that failure to carry out his demands will result in persecution by a young man, far worse than he, who will search out his prey no matter what precautions are taken. The man, as Pip discovers next day, is Compeyson. Later in the novel, all Pip's care in hiding Magwitch and planning of an escape proves useless against Compeyson's evil desires.

Question 4.
How does the novel's structure emphasize the development of Pip's expectations?

Answer
There are three movements in the action of *Great Expectations*. The first (Chapters 1-19) recounts Pip's gradual development from acceptance to rejection of self; the second (Chapters 20-39) traces his movement from a fanciful world of illusion to total disillusionment; the third (Chapters 40-59) recounts his increasing perception of reality and re-acceptance of self. In genre the novel is a *Bildungsroman* (a novel of development which traces the evolving personality and insight of the protagonist from innocence to maturity); it begins with a young boy's innocence and acceptance of the hardship of isolation, and it ends with a mature man's acceptance of a world which, if not the best, is at least sufficient to inhabit with dignity.

In each of the three sections Pip's expectations are, either with or without his knowledge, in conflict with the expectations of another character. In section one, Pip treats Joe "as a larger species of child, and as no more than |his| equal." Their mutual expectation is that somehow Mrs. Joe will be tolerated, Pip will be apprenticed to Joe, and they will share a life of "larks." In the middle of this section Pip is introduced to Satis House. It is the exact opposite to the forge: the former has — by the force of Miss Havisham — stopped time and, like the brewery beside it, "will stand as idle as it is, till it falls;" the latter has — by the force of Joe — been developed from a place of trade neglected by his father to a productive place in which pride can be taken. Miss Havisham's expectations for Pip conflict with Joe's. Pip chooses, and by the end of Chapter 13 he is sure that he can never be happy in Joe's trade. Jaggers appears at the end of the section; he carries with him news that marks the beginning of another's disguised expectations: Magwitch's desire to make of Pip a gentleman.

In section two Pip's vanity leads to his construction of an unexamined world of illusion. His expectations now concern his belief that Estella is meant for him. Again, his expectations are contrasted with Miss Havisham's, the latter's being a desire that Pip — along with as many men as possible — will suffer at Estella's hand. However, the distinguishing feature in the second section is that Pip — through Herbert's explicit and repeated warning — is made aware of the fact that his and Miss Havisham's expectations contrast; moreover, Estella herself warns Pip that his desire will be unfulfilled. Pip blindly proceeds, never realizing that he is caught in a maze of others' expectations. The second section is also distinguished from the first by the quality of Miss Havisham's triumph. Completely triumphant previously over Joe's expectations, she has every reason to believe such will again be the case. However, the original great expectation which had been thwarted (marriage to Compeyson) has flawed her reason; she expects love from a creation (Estella) which she herself constructed so as to be unable to respond to any emotional appeal. Pip's expectations, of course, vanish with the appearance of Magwitch.

In the third section Pip sees Estella married, comes to know her heritage, and realizes the insanity of Miss Havisham and the dignity of Joe. His expectations are no longer self-centered; he merely wishes to execute successfully the escape of Magwitch from London. This expectation is pitted against that of Compeyson, who both fears Magwitch and expects a reward for his capture. Unlike the two earlier sections, Pip is now aware both that another's expectations contrast with his own and that the other (Compeyson) is aware of the contrast. Again Pip fails, but in displaying sincere humanity as he had long ago on the marshes he reclaims the self he had earlier denied.

Characters

Methods of Analyzing Characters

1. Relation of Character to Plot

Aristotle, in describing character as secondary to plot, says: "Character gives us qualities, but it is in actions — what we do — that we are happy or the reverse." He implies an opposition between plot and character which modern literary theorists have rejected on numerous grounds, most notably by attacking Aristotle's supporting thesis that all human emotions, whether happiness or misery, "take the form of action." Many psychological novelists have accepted — though few have publicly done so — Arnold Bennett's statement, which exactly contradicts Aristotle's: "The foundation of good fiction is character creating and nothing else." Perhaps a compromise can be reached by accepting the fact that plot and character exist in a literary work as mutually related verbal carriers of meaning. A careful operation may separate them, but the patient will usually die. To paraphrase a statement by Henry James, plot grows out of character; character grows out of plot. The reader of a good novel may assume that the events recounted will follow logically from the natures of various characters as they interact one with the other. He may therefore begin an appraisal of characterization by examining the motivation for actions.

2. Methods of Characterization

Broadly considered, characters may be revealed in two ways: (1) explicitly or directly: that is, the character is pictured in an expository manner; he is psychologically analyzed; he is described by the narrator;

or another character in the work speaks of his character; and (2) implicitly or indirectly: that is, when the reader is required to make a judgment of a character by listening to him speak, seeing him act, observing the effect he has on other characters, and noting the kind of environment he accepts, chooses, or rejects. If the narrator or character is dependable (and the reader must consider this closely), explicit characterization avoids ambiguity and instantly establishes character clearly. Implicit characterization, on the other hand, makes large demands on the reader and is generally employed to a greater degree when the author intends his character to be ambiguous or his novel to retain heightened suspense. In the case of explicit character delineation by an unreliable narrator or character, the reader is often forced to judge the character's actions and come to a conclusion opposed to that presented explicitly. A reader must have judgment rather than opinions; to have these he must determine how he knows what he holds to be true.

3. Developed and Undeveloped Characters

Requirements of length, intention, and clarity demand that all characters in a novel shall not be fully developed. Developed characters are called "round," "full," or "complete;" undeveloped characters are called "flat," "thin," or "type." A round character is changed by the interaction between himself with his environment and the events of which he is a part. Usually his nature, appearance, environment, habits, emotions, desires, and instincts are presented in detail; then a particular quality is shown to dominate, and that quality comes into conflict with either his own other qualities, his environment, another character or characters, or the events in which he takes part. A flat character, on the other hand, is the same at the end of the novel as at the beginning; he experiences — but he does not change. Quite often he is representative or symbolic; on other occasions he is a device (as, for example, a confidant whose conversation with a full character the reader is permitted to overhear); on still other occasions he simply blends as a part of the backdrop before which an action takes place. The purely flat character is either uncomplicated or the author chooses to make his complications no part of the novel; in any case, he can always be adequately described in a phrase or sentence. The reader of a novel should, first, determine the round characters, then determine what function the flat characters perform in terms of the novel's development.

4. Thematic Characters

Though it is less often true of either major or round characters, numerous minor characters in novels act as they do because they are representative of themes in the novel. The cause of Compeyson's evil, for example, is never explained in terms of his heritage; he is simply a villain. A major theme in the novel is that of persecution, and Compeyson's every act is meant to harm, to harass, to distress, or to oppress — and ultimately to destroy. Since a case can probably be made that every character is in some sense representative, the term "thematic character" should be reserved for a character who clearly represents a dominant abstraction which is clashing with another, i.e., freedom and persecution, love and hate. The reader should carefully analyze the function of such characters. He will likely note their tendency to clarify relationships or to force other characters to act in such a way that ambiguities are clarified.

Character Sketches

Pip

Pip is the protagonist of the novel. He is an imaginative boy (age seven when the novel opens, according to Dickens' notes) who grows fearful and lonely both because of his isolation from normal family ties and because of the oppressiveness of the atmosphere in the marsh country where he lives. As an orphan, he has no expectations, but because of Joe's kindness he is taken in, cared for, and permitted to anticipate following Joe's footsteps as his apprentice. Joe's childlike humility, kindness, and understanding stand in sharp contrast to other early influences on Pip: Mrs. Joe, who considers herself a martyr for marrying a blacksmith and who takes great pride in raising her young brother "by hand;" Uncle Pumblechook, a self-seeking grain merchant whose hypocrisy is thinly veiled; and the other townspeople, who seldom fail to allude to Pip's inferior origins and to the unlikeliness that he will be properly grateful.

Perhaps because he is often accused of ingratitude in his youth, Pip remains throughout the novel periodically conscience-stricken. Because of his imaginative character and deprived state he consistently builds illusions of success on improper evidence, then proceeds to become a snob because of the pride he takes in those illusions. He aspires to education merely for the social status it will provide and, after moderate success, becomes a spend-thrift and joins a prestigious but useless club, called the Finches of the Grove, for young Regency gentlemen.

In the first section of the novel, the reader's pity for Pip gradually fades as the boy's pride becomes more dominant; in the second section Pip's snobbery and conviction of the accuracy of his illusions are despicable; and in the final section he regains the reader's admiration because of his diligent pursuit of truth, his refusal to use evidence to destroy the woman who has given him such misery, his loyalty to

Magwitch, his humble attempts to compensate for the injustices he has dealt Joe and Biddy, and his self-reliant rise from total destruction to moderate business success.

Joe Gargery

Joe is a character whose life serves as a moral standard opposed to all that Pip becomes during the period of his great expectations. The son of a drunken and shiftless father whose wife died early because of mistreatment, Joe married Mrs. Joe and tolerates her "Ram-pages" because he fears the possibility of ever following his father's example in mistreating his wife. He is a blacksmith, a successful craftsman who aspires to no more than filling with pride and dignity his particular role in society. Although uncomfortable in church where he must wear clothes foreign to his work at the forge, Joe is — in Pip's words — a "gentle, Christian man" whose life is so "holy" that it adds a "sanctity" to the house and forge. His speech is low but has far more dignity than the rhetoric of Wopsle or the self-acclaim of Pumblechook. He is uncomfortable in London, rejects quietly all snobbery and falsity; yet he is charitable, forgiving of personal insult and ingratitude, and has little conception of property. Though Pip later perceives Joe's solid honesty and moral depth, he spends his childhood considering him a youthful counterpart: "a mild, good-natured, sweet-tempered, easy going, foolish, dear fellow." Sound intuition into people and situations, good sense, and native sensitiveness and good taste characterize Joe in spite of his apparent superficial slowness.

Mrs. Joe

"A veritable Tarter," Mrs. Joe was more than twenty when Pip was born and his mother died, and "established a great reputation with herself and her neighbors because she had brought |Pip| up 'by hand' . . . a large and heavy hand." She is tall and bony, with black hair and eyes and red skin. Joe refers to her as a fine figure of a woman, but she is not good-looking, and Pip has the impression that "she must have made Joe Gargery marry her by hand."

She has a shrewish temper and pushes Pip and Joe about both figuratively and literally, making life at the forge a burden by complaining of all the hard work she has to do and wearing her coarse apron all the time as a sort of badge of martyrdom. She works hard at unnecessary chores and picks harsh quarrels. Joe describes her outbursts of rage as "going on the Ram-page"; her favorite weapon is "Tickler," a well-worn cane. "She was never polite unless there was company;" but when there is, she unlocks a special store of graciousness.

In the end her temper proves her own undoing; so meanly does she torment Orlick, that one day when she is alone he attacks her murderously, paralyzing her limbs, and affecting her speech. Thereafter she is unnaturally gentle, showing a great desire to pacify Orlick on all occasions. She speaks the word "Pardon" to poor Joe only at the moment of her death, when she also mentions the name of Pip.

George Gissing, the novelist, says of Mrs. Joe:

> Mrs. Gargery belongs to Dickens' later manner . . . his hand was inimitably true . . . though he still disguises the worst of the situation with his unfailing humor, Dickens gives more of the harsh truth than in any previous book . . . there is a fine scene where the woman, by a malicious lie, causes a fight . . . a true illustration of character, and well brought out.

Biddy

An orphan girl, Biddy is the grand-daughter of Mr. Wopsle's great-aunt. Like Pip, she is brought up by hand. She teaches Pip to read. After Orlick's attack on Pip's sister she goes to look after the disabled woman and the Gargery home. Here she continues to help Pip improve in his studies and shows sensitive and wise understanding of his problems and personality. Pip is unable to perceive Biddy's love for himself. She does not attempt to make him see it, and does not even reproach him for his condescension when he finally leaves for London.

Later she goes to live with the Hubbles and becomes the village schoolmistress. She finally marries Joe.

"Biddy was the wisest of girls . . . her hand . . . was a comfortable hand . . . a soothing way. . . ." It is natural for people to go to her, as Pip does, with confidences:

> All that Biddy said seemed right . . . Biddy was never insulting, or capricious, nor Biddy today and somebody else tomorrow; she would have derived only pain, and no pleasure, from giving me pain . . . .

It is natural that Pip, humbled and repentant, should again turn to her in the hope that she will " . . . go through the world with me, |and| . . . make it a better world for me, and me a better man for it . . . ."

Abel Magwitch (Provis)

Magwitch tells his life story in Chapter XLII of the novel. "In jail and out of jail:" this, according to him, is a summary of his life. An orphan with no notion where he was born, his first memory is of stealing turnips for a living. Since then, he can remember only a series of persecutions: jails, being carted about and put out of town, being put in stocks and whipped. A ragged boy whose ugly features always frightened people, he early earned the reputation of being "hardened." His occupations included a bit of work — but principally being a tramp, beggar, and thief. Though he acquired some education, he spent most of his time at things which brought little money yet quickly got him into trouble.

Though Magwitch makes no attempt to disguise his criminality, he is presented by Dickens as emotionally two-sided. As Magwitch, he is persecuted, bent on vengeance (especially toward the villain Compeyson, whose guise as a gentleman has caused Magwitch such suffering), and frightful in appearance; as Provis, he makes a fortune, attempts to repay Pip for the one benevolent act he has ever received, and appears (during the escape attempt) even calmer and less conscious of persecution than Pip. While in making Pip a gentleman he hopes by proxy to experience a life he hasn't lived, his rewards (for example, seeing Pip in a coach and hearing him read aloud in a foreign language) are in fact small. The pleasures he derives from Pip are certainly less malicious than the joys Miss Havisham expects to experience through Estella's actions.

Estella

The adopted daughter of Miss Havisham and heroine of this story, Estella proves to be the daughter of Abel Magwitch, Pip's warmhearted convict, and of Molly, Mr. Jaggers' housekeeper. Miss Havisham asked Mr. Jaggers to find her a child to adopt at the time when Molly, on trial for murder, was persuaded to give up her baby to be brought up in safety. Miss Havisham brought the child up as an instrument for her revenge on men in general. She was to break their hearts while remaining indifferent.

Estella is a girl of delicate beauty and immense poise. From the time when Pip meets her when both are children he is fascinated and disturbed by her. She changes his whole outlook to one of dissatisfaction with his "common" lot. Though she makes him wretched, he feels he can not live without her. Her training and her maturing beauty make her seem more and more unattainable, although Miss Havisham deliberately throws her in Pip's way and expresses her intention that he should escort her around London.

Her decision to marry the brutal Drummle is an odd one. Social position may appear to be the bait, but she must know that all Miss Havisham's wealth is at her disposal. Perhaps she does it as a gesture of scorn for the romantic notion of marrying for love. She lacks any trace of warmth of feeling, even for her foster mother, and explains her attitude as dutifulness and a successful following-up of her teaching.

The cruelty of her husband changes her, by a process we are not shown at all, into a more sympathetic person. In the original ending she and Pip meet in a park and greet each other with sadness, but as circumstances do not permit their coming together they pass on, each into lonely melancholy. In the final version, both are free; without much expressed response on her part, she leaves the scene with Pip. Though her manner implies friendship and deeper feeling, the reader is left to fill in further details of the change for himself.

Miss Havisham

Like the house and surroundings she inhabits, Miss Havisham is crumbling with age. As a girl, she had been proud, rich, and determined. Her father, a brewer, had secretly married and had a son (Arthur) by his cook. The son was wild and, because of his numerous escapades, led his father to disinherit him (though the father later partially altered his decision and left the son a small fortune which was soon squandered), thus leaving Miss Havisham an heiress of great wealth. By all she was considered a great marriage prospect; however, she chose a handsome and apparent gentleman named Compeyson, an "operator" to whom all her relatives except Matthew Pocket were too "toady" to object. Compeyson, promising to marry her, was secretly in league with the partially disinherited half-brother; he managed to play on her emotions and thereby fraudulently acquire control of much of her wealth. On the presumed wedding day — with the feast laid out and the bride dressing — he sent a cutting note which ended Miss Havisham's expectations of happiness.

When the novel opens, the events of Miss Havisham's life are apparently town gossip, but they happened in the distant past. For Miss Havisham, however, time stopped with the receipt of Compeyson's note: all clocks at Satis House are stopped at the moment; the yellowed wedding dress still hangs on her emaciated figure; and the wedding feast, rotted and bug-infested, still lies on the table where Miss Havisham says she will be laid after her death.

Miss Havisham is clearly mad (as Pip recognizes after Magwitch's return). By refusing to entertain any of the healing influences from the outside world, she has permitted her mind to conceive a malignant and self-centered revenge. She raises Estella to be the weapon to achieve her revenge, and just as Magwitch turned Pip upside down in the churchyard, she bequeaths on her protegée a value system which is inverted and inhuman: coldness, sarcasm, and enticement are its virtues. Her obsessed mind, like Dr. Frankenstein's, fails to recognize that the created monster may sometime turn on its creator; years later she pleads for Estella's love — only to be told that Estella cannot give that which she does not possess.

Miss Havisham's deranged mind manipulates details with precision: she takes advantage of Pip's ignorance of the source of his expectations; she uses him both as an object on whom Estella may practise her cruel charms and as a way of antagonizing her greedy relatives. Later, however, she is able to go beyond her malignant desires and see the damage she has done: Estella's unhappiness and Pip's wrecked hopes. With moving humility, she begs forgiveness and soon thereafter dies. It is only after her death, after all her property is sold and no part of the house remains, after her influence over Estella has been broken by suffering, that Pip and Estella can meet again on the grounds where Satis House once stood.

Mr. Jaggers

Jaggers is a brilliant and overbearing criminal lawyer with the astounding capacity of always seeming to be right, and an air of always knowing something secret about everybody with whom he deals.

"He was a burly man of an exceedingly dark complexion, with an exceedingly large head and a corresponding large hand." His shaven chin is very dark, and he has an odd habit of biting the side of his great forefinger, and of "throwing it" in a half-bullying sort of way, at the person he is talking with. His hands always smell of scented soap, from his conscientious washing of them after any contact with his clients and the courts and jails.

Mr. Jaggers' office and his home are both grim and matter-of-fact to the least detail, expressing not the smallest sign of relaxation. The main decoration of the office seems to be the pair of plaster masks of two of the lawyer's clients made after they were taken down from the gallows, and the wreaths carved in the panelling of his diningroom remind Pip of hangman's nooses.

He is "Deep . . . as Australia." Though he would throw out of his office anyone who indicated that he had feelings, he is a man of deeply suppressed feelings himself. He reveals real feeling on the one occasion that he is startled by Pip's outburst about the parentage of Estella. He sighs just once at the thought of relaxing in a comfortable atmosphere; then he outlines the "hypothetical" case of the "one pretty child out of the heap that could be saved." He implies that he knows what it is to have youthful dreams. Probably it is human compassion for the old convict that makes him try to get his trial put off until it is too late for human justice to touch him. Speaking of Jaggers, Gissing says:

> The legal world of his day . . . Dickens painted from nature
> . . . and with an artist's love of his subject . . . we watch the
> grim gravity of Mr. Jaggers with entire conviction. In this department of his work Dickens can be said to idealize only in the sense of the finest art; no praise can exaggerate his dexterity in setting forth these examples of supreme realism . . . .
> The clerks are as much alive as their employers. . . .Jaggers and Wemmick would make a novelist's reputation.

John Wemmick

Chief clerk to Mr. Jaggers, Mr. Wemmick is a man between forty and fifty years old, dry, and rather short in stature. He has a square wooden face whose expression seems to have been imperfectly chipped out with a dull-edged chisel.

At work, Wemmick is merely a piece of legal machinery, ever concerned with "portable property." He is a shrewd judge of character and business, gets on well with his employer, is ashamed to show his feelings, and deals capably with Mr. Jaggers' clients. It is he who pays Pip his allowance.

At home in Walworth, he is a different man: fond of his deaf and aged father, ingenious in devising gadgets for his tiny castle with its drawbridge, moat and cannon, and partial to the stiff Miss Skiffins around whose waist he tries to slip his arm. Dickens brings out the humanity of officialdom with his description of Wemmick's Walworth life, and creates much humor by means of Wemmick, as in the wedding incident.

Herbert Pocket

The eldest son of Matthew Pocket, Herbert becomes a warm friend of Pip. He and Pip first meet at Miss Havisham's house, where Herbert launches into a fist-fight with the unwilling but physically stronger Pip. They part with no hard feelings, for Herbert is a mild and friendly soul and a good sport. When Pip comes to London he is astonished to find that the young gentleman with whom he is to share rooms and learn how young gentlemen behave is the same "pale young gentleman." Pip describes Herbert in a kindly manner:

> Herbert Pocket had a frank and easy way with him that was very taking. I have never seen anyone since who more strongly expressed to me, in every look and tone, a natural incapacity to do anything secret or mean. There was something wonderfully hopeful about his general air, and something that at the same time whispered to me that he would never be successful or rich.

Herbert has plans as big as the East India Company, but reveals that he has not even a job yet that pays him money: only one that gives him an opportunity for "looking about." He is a good judge of other people, from his own snobbish mother to his associates and to Estella, whom he recognizes as "hard, haughty and capricious to the last degree, having been brought up . . . to wreak vengeance on all the male sex." He sees at once Pip's infatuation with Estella, and suggests that Pip would be saved possible "miserable things" by detaching himself from her. He sees quickly how Provis is likely to behave if disappointed

107

in the response of "his gentleman," and shows both loyalty and common-sense in working out the necessary course to be followed. This same devotion to the interests of his friend is carried even further in his rescue of Pip from Orlick, in his steadiness during the attempted escape, and in his conscientious work in the firm of Clarriker. In his romantic life, also, Herbert is simple, conscientious and devoted, and apparently happy in his modest home.

Uncle Pumblechook

A well-to-do corn and seed merchant. Uncle Pumblechook has a house in Pip's nearest town. He has power in the family because of his wealth and importance.

Actually Joe's uncle, he is appropriated by Mrs. Joe. His outstanding characteristics are his pomposity and self-importance and his hypocrisy. He torments the younger Pip by ruffling his hair and lecturing him about gratitude. When Pip is a little older, Pumblechook recommends him to Miss Havisham, whose tenant he is. When Pip quite unexpectedly comes into his "great expectations," "that fearful imposter" struts about, pretending to be the originator of his good fortune, and becomes as flattering as he had been tyrannical. When Pip meets with a reversal of fortune Pumblechook becomes insultingly compassionate: "Windy donkey as he was, it really amazed me that he could have the face to talk thus," Pip says of him.

Pumblechook is one of the sharpest expressions of Dickens' unrelenting scorn of humbug, hypocrisy and meanness of soul. Gissing remarks:

> . . . That rich little book, *Great Expectations,* contains a humbug . . . on the surface greatly amusing, but illustrative of a contemptible quality closely allied to the commercial spirit. Seen at a distance Mr. Pumblechook is a source of inextinguishable laughter; near at hand he is seen to be a very sordid creature . . . Here we have a form of dishonesty peculiar to no one people . . . Compare him with |Dickens'| other embodiments of dishonesty, and it is seen, not only that inexhaustible material of this kind lay at Dickens' command, but with what excellent art he differentiates his characters.

Mr. Wopsle

Parish clerk in the Gargery's village, Mr. Wopsle would like to be a clergyman, but is not of the right social class. He has a Roman nose, a rich voice of which he is very proud, and strong dramatic instincts. He tries to outdo his clergyman in reading the service, and seizes every opportunity to read poetry, Shakespeare, and murder trial reports.

Frustrated by the insignificance of his own village, he leaves it for the stage in a fourth-rate London theater, and changes his name to Waldengarver. Pip and Herbert go to see him as Hamlet — a grotesque exhibition of "ham" acting — and find that "Mr. Wopsle had not succeeded in reviving the Drama, but, on the contrary, had rather partaken of its decline."

Orlick

He is a journeyman employed by Joe Gargery, and becomes Pip's bitter enemy. He is described in very sinister terms:

> He was a broad-shouldered, loose-limbed, swarthy fellow of great strength . . . always slouching . . . He never seemed to come to work on purpose, but would slouch in as if by mere accident . . . or to the Jolly Bargeman . . . or home at night . . . like Cain of the Wandering Jew, as if he had no idea where he was going and no intention of ever coming back. He lodged at a sluicekeeper's out on the marshes . . . He always slouched, locomotively, with his eyes on the ground; and when accosted . . . he looked up in a resentful, half-puzzled way . . . .

He has rather a sharp and sarcastic tongue. The day he wheedles a half-holiday out of Joe, his shrewd and insulting summing-up of Mrs. Joe leads to a fight, and Joe has to thrash him. The upshot is a murderous attack on Mrs. Joe, for which, however, he does not get the blame.

This wretched creature is attracted to Biddy whom he haunts silently, sometimes "dancing at" her, sometimes watching her from the branches of a tree, and hating Pip the more for interfering.

Later he leaves the forge to be employed by Miss Havisham as a watchman. Pip's influence with Jaggers leads to the removal of so dubious a guardian. His hatred of Pip grown still stronger for this, he falls under the influence of Compeyson, whom he helps to shadow Pip and Provis. He finally entices Pip to a lonely sluice-house on the marsh and torments him as a preliminary to a savage and revengeful murder. His plan is interrupted, though, by the arrival of Pip's friends. At last he is put in the county jail for breaking into the house of Mr. Pumblechook.

Bentley Drummle

A sulky, old-looking young man from a good country family, Drummle is full of contempt for his fellow pupils at Mr. Pocket's home. Heavy in figure, movement and comprehension, he is idle, proud, stingy, reserved, suspicious, and chronically ill-at-ease. He is, from the first, Pip's enemy, even before they argue over Estella. Mr.

Jaggers finds him an interesting criminal study, and calls him The Spider.

Estella marries him, perhaps for the sake of his position and wealth, but more likely out of indifference or spite. He beats and otherwise mistreats her, separates from her, and finally meets his death when he is kicked by a horse he used brutally. He is the agent by whom Estella is humanized.

Chart: Character Delineation

	Pip	Joe	Pumblechook	Miss Havisham
Character type	imaginative; potential snob	contented master crafts-man	pretentious and overbearing; social climber and tradesman	rejected lover who becomes neurotic
Central motiva-tion	expectations	trust in ultimate good of Pip	prudent self-interest	revenge and (later) regret
Principal action(s)	rejects both world of childhood and delusions of youth	frees Pip from appren-ticeship bond and remains faithful to him	effects Pip's meeting with Miss Havisham and flatters or deprecates all with con-sideration of his own in-terests	deludes Pip and makes of Estella a heartless monster
Principal emotion(s) and at-tributes	snobbery and love	humility, contentment, and love	desire for public esteem and hypocrisy	pain from being re-jected and its resultant hardness
Condition at begin-ning of novel	isolated child with expecta-tion of ap-prenticeship	successful craftsman, married to shrew	semi-successful tradesman	emaciated spinster for whom time has stopped
Condition at end of novel	mature man who accepts limited suc-cess	successful craftsman with a wife and children whose characters match his own	comically deflated at hands of Orlick	dead after dramatic repentance and forgiveness

Estella	Orlick	Magwitch	Jaggers
beautiful and heartless automaton	bestial criminal and villain; journeyman	fated criminal	self-confident and respected lawyer
Miss Havisham's desires	animal lust and revenge	devotion to Pip and hate for Compeyson	sense of universal justice
torments and rejects Pip in favor of Drummle, who breaks her heart by intensive mistreatment	kills Mrs. Joe, aids Compeyson, attempts to kill Pip, and deflates Pumblechook	unintentionally makes Pip a snob by trying to repay Pip's former kindness	serves as Pip's guardian
without emotion	revengeful lack of principles	gratitude to Pip and sense of injustice suffered	unemotional devotion to power and evidence
heartless child	journeyman employed by Joe and living in marshes	pursued criminal	successful lawyer
mature woman, emotionally responsive as result of suffering	arrested through Pumblechook's identification	dead after receiving Pip's complete devotion	successful lawyer

Questions and Answers on the Characters

Question 5.

To what extent is Pip's moral position defined by his relation to flat characters?

Answer

Three groups of flat characters function essentially as devices to define Pip's moral position. Most notable of these groups is the one which includes Pip's confidants: Biddy, Herbert, and Wemmick. Though they are respectively the people to whom Pip verbalizes his intentions during the three stages of his expectations, they are also the educators who widen his comprehension of their respective social circles. Biddy alone contributes to Pip's formal education; more significantly, she teaches him that pride and dignity can be derived from filling one's place at the forge as well as from the possession of money and prestige. That Pip does not immediately accept the lessons foreshadows the continuing blindness which results in his mistreatment of Joe and affiliation with the Finches of the Grove. Once Pip arrives in London, Biddy's role as educator and confidante is taken over by Herbert. As an instructor, Herbert resembles his father Matthew: he teaches both by what he says and by what he is. Verbally, he corrects Pip's manners, provides him with background information relative to Miss Havisham's circle and her intentions, and introduces him to London life; by his actions, he demonstrates a determined pursuit of an idealistic — and seemingly impossible — goal. With all Herbert has to offer, Pip learns only those things which contribute to his building for himself the facade of a gentleman. He refuses to heed warnings about Estella and Miss Havisham, and he mistakes (as he admits years later) Herbert's cheerful industry and readiness for unworldly incompetence. Dickens carefully prepares for Wemmick's assuming the role of confidant and educator by placing Herbert in the background — giving him a job, a complicated romance, and a necessary trip to Cairo. Among criminals Wemmick moves like a gardener among plants; thus it is fitting that he should be Pip's tutor in the final stage of his expectations, since there Pip is most concerned with the motives and methods of criminals. By first informing Pip that his chambers are watched and then suggesting a course of action, Wemmick implies the complications which Pip had not yet anticipated. Moreover, he clarifies Estella's nature by describing the character of her mother and thus furnishing evidence which leads to recognition that Magwitch is the girl's father. He suggests that "portable property" is endangered by Pip's rejection of Miss Havisham's offer and the situation with Magwitch. The regaining of Pip's assertive and forceful character is demonstrated by the fact that he is pitted against a foe (Compeyson) the villainy of whom even

Wemmick — an expert in dealing with criminals — cannot fathom. After the failure of the escape attempt, Wemmick apologizes — claims that he tried his best to be of service — and concludes that it was a part of Compeyson's "policy, as a very clever man, habitually to deceive his own instruments." By Wemmick's marriage, Pip recognizes that the duality of existence entertained both by him and by Jaggers is a feasible one. He can himself now be a productive citizen and accept — though it may not be ideal — a role in a "tainted" social order.

The second group of flat characters are opposite in action but serve a common function: revelation of the weakness and negation of self in the pose Pip assumes during the period of his great expectations. Pumblechook is a parasite; in hopes of enhancing his own position and esteem, he flatters every person of wealth or power whose path he crosses — especially Pip. Trabb's boy is a deflater of hypocrites; with no concern for his own position at Trabb's business, he wittily and boldly deflates Pip's pose. As a young boy, Pip had been aware of Pumblechook's pose; he now finds Trabb's boy in the position he had once occupied, and ironically he is himself the stuffed shirt acting Pumblechook's role. Such a role negates force of character: "But unless I had taken the life of Trabb's boy on that occasion, I really do not even now see what I could have done save endure. To have struggled with him in the street, or to have exacted any lower recompense from him than his heart's best blood, would have been futile and degrading." Pip's idea of honor — like Pumblechook's — has no relation to morality; he is concerned with how he appears in the eyes of others, not with the moral significance of his actions. In writing Trabb and in using his own wealth to avenge himself and throw the boy's position in jeopardy, Pip does less than exact "his heart's best blood." As he had himself judged, the act is "futile and degrading;" but he is unconcerned since it is not committed before the eyes of others.

Orlick and Drummle, both flat thematic characters whose unrestrained savage power is opposed to Pip's weakness, merge into a single character who represents bestial force in two levels of society. One should note that the appearance of the two is quite similar; moreover, after Pip's verbal confrontation with Drummle and just before his belatedly forceful approach to Estella, he sees Drummle and Orlick together. Orlick parallels Pip in action: he is a worker at the forge; he is insulted by Mrs. Joe and attracted by Biddy; he goes from the forge to Miss Havisham's; and he goes from Satis House to London where he assists a former criminal. Once established in London, Pip finds a parallel in Drummle: Drummle rows behind Pip and his confidant Herbert as Orlick had walked behind Pip and his confidante Biddy; Drummle threatens to strike Startop as Orlick had struck Mrs. Joe; Drummle and Pip study under a common teacher, attend Jaggers' party together, and belong to the same club; they both are attracted to Estella and appear at the same time at the Blue Boar with the intention of seeing her. Together the desires and achievements of Orlick-Drummle place Pip's powerlessness in a clear light: Orlick attacks Mrs. Joe, at whose hands Pip had also suffered; Orlick's interest in Biddy is sexual, Pip's platonic; Orlick pursues a career at Satis House, Pip has one cast upon him; Orlick pursues Pip and joins Compeyson; Pip pines away for Estella, while Drummle beats her into submission. Because Orlick and Drummle are instinctively criminal, they devote little effort to disguising themselves. Pip's desires, though at times criminal, are submerged and rendered impossible by the disguise he assumes.

Question 6.

What methods are employed in developing Miss Havisham's character?

Answer

Dickens employs both the explicit and implicit modes in developing the character of Miss Havisham. Moreover, the suggestions which appear concerning Miss Havisham's character — since few specific details are known until after Pip meets Herbert in London — create an aura of mystery about her. Only two facts relative to her are presented explicitly in the first section: Pip relates that common gossip about town describes her ''as an immensely rich and grim lady who lived in a large and dismal house barricaded against robbers, and who led a life of seclusion,'' and he describes her grotesque appearance on the occasion of his first visit to Satis House. More significant, however, are the details which permit the reader to infer certain things about her. The excited behavior of Mrs. Joe and Pumblechook, when they bring news of Pip's invitation, quickly blends into their assumption that great things may be in store for Pip as a result of the visit. Likewise, though they are usually suspicious, they apparently are so much in the dark concerning Miss Havisham that they willingly believe Pip's tall tales about the events of his visit. On that first visit, he notes details which only much later fall into place: Miss Havisham's failure to receive Pumblechook, the appearance of her room, the moment at which timepieces are stopped, her reference to a broken heart and whispered comment to Estella concerning the breaking of Pip's heart, the absence of natural light, her permitting Estella to taunt Pip rudely, and later her intense questioning of his reaction to Estella. On Pip's second visit, he again notes numerous details: the room in which dust and mold cover a long tablecloth, Miss Havisham's comment that she will be buried there, the behavior of Miss Havisham's relatives and her reaction to them, the strange allusion to Matthew, her reference to a bride's dress and a horrible event which took place before Pip's birth, and the appearance of a strange young gentleman. Subsequent visit bring more details, the most notable of which is Miss Havisham's reaction to her relatives as she acts so as to sustain Pip's belief that she is his benefactress.

During the second and third stages of Pip's expectations, explicit characterization is used to a far greater extent. Herbert relates both the details of Miss Havisham's youth leading up to the destructive affair with Compeyson and the course that her revenge is taking in relation to Estella. Jaggers later explains his part in filling her request for a young girl to raise, and Magwitch's monologue presents Compeyson in a clear light. Besides these judgments by other characters, Pip himself psychologically analyzes Miss Havisham after he has gained additional details by watching her plead for Estella's love and for his forgiveness.

Though Dickens' method in cumulatively building a full portrait of Miss Havisham firmly impresses her on the reader's consciousness, it is not entirely successful. In the case of Estella, the transformation takes place offstage and thus the suddenness of her reversal does not appear to lack motivation — especially since the reader is aware of Drummle's force and Jaggers' appreciation of it. However, there is really no preparation for Miss Havisham's change from malignant joy to sorrow for her actions. That the transformation takes place onstage results in the lack of preparation being all the more obvious. The sudden rounding of a character whose flatness has been suggested by numerous characterizing devices is unfortunate.

Question 7.

Briefly describe Jaggers' role within the novel.

Answer

Jaggers acts both as a device serving the structure of the novel and as a moral (he would prefer "prudent") agent enforcing the meaning of the novel. As a device he makes possible the following narrative situations: (1) Magwitch's secret role as Pip's benefactor; (2) Miss Havisham's collecting enough details of Pip's relationship with his benefactor to lead both Pip and her relatives to believe she is the actual source of his expectations; and (3) Miss Havisham's acquiring of a foster child and Pip's later awareness of the details concerning it.

As a moral force, Jaggers demonstrates the fact that confusions between illusion and reality bear tragic consequences. Trust evidence only, never appearance, opinion, or emotion: this is his motto. The reader first becomes aware of his rhetorical powers when he destroys Wopsle's arbitrary assumption of the guilt of an accused murderer. That the judicial system actually relies too heavily on appearance is demonstrated by the treatment of Magwitch as compared to that of Compeyson in the two trials. The reader should note, however, that Jaggers is not only attorney for the innocent damned; he is also defender of the guilty. An astute observer, he only gives up a case when *evidence* is insurmountable. If, on the other hand, he can bully a jury, confuse a judge, frighten a witness — all these he will do even if he knows his client to be guilty (as in the case of Molly, Estella's mother). How, then, can we say Jaggers is a *moral* force? The answer is that he recognizes that class barriers have, through the years, established a situation in which appearances lead to judgment of guilt and in which the environment of the poor (as in the case of Magwitch) forces them to criminal acts. In effect, Jaggers balances the scales of a higher justice than that embodied in the law.

Meaning

Methods of Analyzing Meaning

A critic once said in jest that "The Rime of the Ancient Mariner" is a "tract written by the Bureau of Prevention of Cruelty to Albatrosses." If one could assume that the critic was serious (though one cannot, of course), one would charge him with an excessive desire to find in the poem a didactic or moral intent. Unfortunately, that desire remains a still-living legacy of a time in which literature was considered frivolous — perhaps sinful — unless it clearly contributed to the moral instruction of the reader. Occasionally one still hears students ask: "What is the moral that writer is trying to get across?" While one may not assume that every novelist attempts to teach a lesson or to moralize, he may justifiably search for the meaning of a novel. In a sense, the novelist translates a thought into action by using the form implied in the term *novel*; a reader reverses the process and translates action back into thought. When one analyzes plot, character, style, and technique, one should constantly be aware of discussing, not isolated phenomena, but mutually related verbal constructions which carry a common meaning.

1. Theme
Put most simply, the term "theme" means an attitude or idea expressed by an author toward a subject. Since most novels reveal authorial attitudes and ideas on numerous subjects, it is self-evident that most novels have numerous themes. However, there is usually a major theme, a prevailing attitude or idea which a great part of the novel tends to illustrate.

2. Defining Thematic Emphasis
There are numerous characteristics of the novel which may indicate degrees of thematic emphasis: (1) characters whose names denote abstract qualities, such as Goodman or Allworthy; (2) characters or settings whose names constitute allusions with fixed meanings, such as Job

or Christmas; (3) plots which recall mythic plots or employ archetypal motifs, such as Faulkner's *A Fable* or Mann's *The Holy Sinner*; (4) settings, isolated and complete, which epitomize the world or serve as a microcosm, such as the *Pequod* in Melville's *Moby-Dick*; (5) traditional images and symbols, such as a white flag, or cross, or a serpent; (6) authorial intrusion to editorialize; (7) judgments expressed by a reliable character or group of characters; or (8) multiple situations which deal with a single attitude or idea, such as the three characters' relations to sin in Hawthorne's *The Scarlet Letter*. In defining theme, the reader must consistently determine how he is led to believe certain ideas, and to distinguish the conventions by which the novelist attains this acceptance.

3. Distinguishing the Book's Value System

To derive objectively the meaning of a novel requires that the reader temporarily *suspend his own stock responses*. The value system of a novelist will likely vary to some degree from that of the reader. The novelist's theme is developed in terms of his value system, and to define that theme the reader must understand — if not accept — the system through which it is developed. For example, if a reader normally is of the opinion that all clergymen are hypocritical and corrupt, he must suspend that prejudice if he is to understand *The Scarlet Letter*. If he considers a military deserter or an unfaithful wife too despicable to be important, he must withhold those responses in order to understand Hemingway's *A Farewell to Arms* or Flaubert's *Madame Bovary*.

After suspending stock responses so as to approach the novel objectively, the reader must attempt to understand the values held by the novelist. Answers to the following questions imply such an understanding: What actions enhance man's worth and what actions depreciate it? What contrasts exist between morality and the ethical conduct of the characters? If there is an ideal existence on earth, what actions by the characters contribute to its not being realized? Of the forces which influence man (supernatural, psychological, external nature, physical health, personal relationship, ancestry, institutions), which exert greatest influence on the plot development? Does any one of those forces exert absolute control over one or all characters in the novel? If characters are controlled by outside forces, do those forces display intention: good, evil, justice, indifference? Is there one characteristic assumed to determine virtue or vice? To what persons or things do the protagonist and antagonist hold allegiance and to which show disloyalty, antipathy, or indifference?

Pip's Changing Reactions to Characters (Chapter Numbers Appear in Parentheses Preceding Entry)

	Joe	Magwitch	Miss Havisham	Estella	Herbert	Pumblechook
First Stage of Expectations (Chapters 1-19)	(2) considers him fellow child and sufferer (4) considers him out of place in Sunday clothes (6) guilt at not confiding (7) gratitude and educational superiority (8) shame for Joe's hearing his lie; how low Estella would find Joe (13) ashamed of Joe's appearance and behavior (15) desires to make him less common (18) resents his sadness and wonder at Pip's new position (19) feels Joe is ungrateful; later regrets attitude	(1) fears grotesque appearance and desperate behavior (3) sympathy (5) sense that no hope remains for him (10) coarse and common for being associated with criminals (16) guilt that file served as weapon against Mrs. Joe (19) comforted that aid to him is long past	(8) surprise at her appearance (9) confounded by her words and actions (12) becomes accustomed to her and able to converse (15) considers her life picturesque (18) considers her his benefactress	(8) hurt and deflated by her treatment of him; "finds her contempt infectious" and manner proud (11) dazzled by her beauty and feels himself more common (14) fears that she will see him at forge (17) confesses verbally his admiration for her (19) hopes she is destined for him	(11) considers him brave and innocent (12) guilt for having beaten him	(4) considers him overbearing and pompous (8) considers him a sadist (9) obstinacy (12) resents his air of proprietorship (19) convinced by flattery that Pumblechook is fine fellow
Second Stage of Expectations (Chapters 20-39)	(27) dreads his visit; disgusted at his bewilderment and formality; regrets attitude toward him (34) realizes neglect of Joe, senses his own loss	(28) dread and fear (39) recognition, repugnance, dread, sense of responsibility for him	(22) curiosity (29) amazed at her command, yet grateful (38) amazed by her scene with Estella (39) recognizes she has deluded him	(22) curiosity (29) considers her both irresistible and intended for him; observes her increased elegance, again feels himself inferior, observes that she lures him	(21) surprised at his identity (22) feels he will never be secret, mean, rich, or successful; considers him a well-mannered dreamer (26) patronizes him	(30) avoids him

Second Stage of Expectations (Chapters 20-39) (Continued)	(35) professes intent to visit him often (39) feels need for him, but hopeless separation			(30) impossible to forget her (32) excitement at seeing her and noting strangeness (33) hopes for her increase (38) recognizes she trusts him familiarly but without favor; amazed at Drummle's toast	(30) decides (if possible) to help him financially (34) notes succumbing to extravagance and despondency (37) through Wemmick Pip arranges for position with Clarriker	(52) realizes his falseness as compared to Joe (58) suffers his insults
Third Stage of Expectations (Chapters 40-59)	(52) realizes his thanklessness (57) realizes his faithfulness and devotion; repentant (58) seeing Joe married to Biddy, thankful did not mention intentions to marry her	(40) considers him horrible and uncouth, yet feels "chained to" him (41) hopes to get him out of England, then break with him (46) notes he has softened; now has genuine concern for his benefactor's welfare (54) totally concerned with his safety; vows never to leave his side (56) senses he is resigned to death; aware of injustice of trial	(44) recognizes her triumph, then her pity and remorse (49) pities her; forgives her; aware of her insanity	(43) decides never to mention her to Magwitch (44) confesses to her his love, but realizes he has lost her (47) feels sure her marriage has taken place (48) reacts to Jaggers' allusion to her marriage; senses Molly is her mother (50) aware Magwitch is her father (51) ambiguous motivation to discover her parentage; confirms truth (59) perceives and accepts her change	(40) relieved by his appearance (49) secures Miss Havisham's help for him (52) aware Herbert must leave for East, thus their separation (58) becomes partner with him	

Questions and Answers on Meaning

Question 8.
Describe the essential meaning of *Great Expectations.*

Answer
In *Great Expectations,* Dickens asserts the vanity of entertaining great expectations in a world where hope is so easily compromised or destroyed. This general statement may be substantiated by briefly recalling the plot and considering it in terms of the novelist's conception of the human situation. Such an examination will reveal that Pip reaches maturity when he can accept a human compromise. He begins as a semi-illiterate apprentice with hopes someday of becoming a craftsman; he ends as a semi-educated clerk who finally becomes a partner in a respectable but not terribly successful business. Objectively, this represents a rise in English society which is partially earned; it falls far short, of course, of Pip's great expectations of wealth, prestige, and a beautiful wife — all compliments of a fairy godmother.

The world of this novel is one in which the great expectations of various characters cannot be fulfilled because they inevitably come into conflict with each other. Just as Miss Havisham's expectation of a happy marriage had been thwarted because it conflicted with the expectations of wealth by the evil Compeyson, so Pip's expectations — which require that his unearned money come from a noble source — are obviously incompatible with those of Magwitch. Morever, in the microcosm created by Dickens no force is provided which untangles knotted expectations and provides success for the deserving. The law is applied by men who are blinded by illusions; and, even if it were not, it is a code devised to support not morality, but an ethical system which defends distinctions of social rank rather than distinctions of human worth.

Question 9.
Distinguish the mutually incompatible value systems in *Great Expectations* which are shown to separate humanity.

Answer
The number of characters in *Great Expectations,* together with the variety of social positions they represent, reveal that Dickens has presented a full microcosm of human values. The persons, things, and ideas to which the various characters favor differ so radically that actions resulting from those preferences inevitably become either confused or result in conflict.

Of all the possible arrangements of contrasts, Joe and Orlick are most clearly opposed. Joe is committed to the validity of social distinctions and to the potential for dignity which rests on every rung of the social ladder. His struggle for excellence is horizontal: it takes place on the level of the master craftsman. Orlick, on the other hand, is committed to nothing but the fulfilment of his bestial desires. Though a journeyman, he bears allegiance to no social group; his actions are never motivated in terms of either morality or ethics.

Pumblechook and Wopsle hold allegiances which are compatible, if not comparable. Pumblechook recognizes the worth of people only in terms of their demonstrated or potential contributions (money, prestige, etc.) to him. Though a tradesman, he has little allegiance to his class (as Pip notices on the morning of his first visit to Satis House). Indifferent to his equals, he verbally abuses those below and is extremely flattering to those above. Wopsle's only allegiance is to an animated and eloquent rhetoric and to those who do or can react with appreciation to his acting.

Miss Havisham, though socially a "lady," bears no allegiance to society's conception of a lady's behavior. Ironically paralleling Pumblechook, she does not consider people for what they are; she evaluates them in terms of potential contribution to her neurotic revenge just as he evaluates them in terms of potential contribution to his wealth and prestige. Only late in the novel does she realize that she has used people just as Compeyson once used her.

Compeyson and Magwitch are criminals; they naturally hold no allegiance to their class. For Compeyson, the abstract presence of honor and humanity is dangerous; safety and success lie in the adoption of a pose. Magwitch, by suffering from both justice's emphasis on punishment and from Compeyson's successful pose, comes to recognize that appearance has greater utilitarian value than does reality. Unlike Compeyson, however, he slowly loses the ability to distinguish between appearance and reality. Unable to be a gentleman himself, he deludes himself into thinking his efforts toward Pip will create a real gentleman, rather than simply an appearance of one. Much more noble than this facet of his aspiration for Pip is another: he bears allegiance to Pip *the person,* a young boy on the marshes whom he will aid because the boy is unique in having treated him with sympathy and humanity.

Jaggers' allegiance is to evidence and power. To him all abstractions (glory, honor, justice, love, etc.) are without meaning because the translation of abstraction into ethical behavior depends on corrupt mankind. He refuses to commit himself on any issue because he is aware that commitment necessitates a position which inevitably has weaknesses. Evidence to him is a source of power; when evidence goes against him, he relies on other sources: rhetoric, emotional appeal, mechanical precision, distortion by manipulation of appearances. Though within the social scale he is a lawyer, he bears no allegiance to the law except as a tool by which he can exert power. In this sense, his allegiance resembles Wemmick's allegiance to "portable property."

The objects of Pip's allegiance alter in the course of the novel. Though at first his resemble Joe's, he soon parallels Pumblechook in desiring money and prestige and then resembles his benefactor's nobler allegiance by devoting himself to the one who had sacrificed so much for him. Because actions based on this shifting allegiance conflict with the actions of others, the novel emphasizes the ineffective nature of human conduct.

Question 10.

Is the theme of child mistreatment a major one in *Great Expectations* as it is in so many of Dickens' novels?

Answer

In other novels of Dickens, most notably *Oliver Twist* and *David Copperfield,* greater length is devoted to the childhood of the protagonist and thus the reader is more firmly impressed by the author's handling of the theme of child mistreatment. Though the hardships which characterized the childhoods of Joe and Magwitch receive brief mention and the neurotic treatment which Estella received may be suggested, the theme of child mistreatment is handled quite generally by Pip's observation of the London criminal scene and by Jaggers' explanation of his role in Estella's becoming Miss Havisham's ward. Only Pip's youth and suffering are handled in any detail, and that emphasis is confined to the first six chapters of a fifty-nine-chapter novel.

Emphasis, then, is not so pronounced in the handling of Pip's childhood mistreatment as it had been in the handling of this theme in earlier novels. Nevertheless, the indignities Pip suffers at an early age and his emotional response to them do recall the persecution of earlier protagonists. Like them, he is an orphan and thus isolated from familiar ties and security; like them, he has no clearly defined position in community which would offer him a source of potential pride. Pip is brought up harshly by a masculine sister who constantly lets him know that her pride results from the community's awareness that she bothers to raise him at all. Self-satisfied and hypocritical adults — such as the Humbles, Pumblechook, and Wopsle — plague him with insult, plant in him a sense of guilt for not being properly grateful to them who raise him "by hand," and consciously neglect providing any word or thing which would contribute to his comfort and pleasure. Thus isolated from family, community, clearly defined future, and anything on which pride could be based, he very early associates himself with death as experienced in the churchyard where his parents and five brothers lie buried. There he becomes aware of himself as a "small bundle of shivers growing afraid of it all and beginning to cry."

123

Unlike several other Dickens heroes, Pip does have one source of strength on which he can always lean. Unfortunately, however, he does not recognize Joe as this strength until he has long passed childhood. During his early years, he considers Joe a child like himself who must also suffer the verbal attacks of Mrs. Joe and the implied insults of the other adults. When he decides against telling Joe of the theft committed to help Magwitch, he does so not — as in the case of the other adults — because he fears humiliation and punishment, but because he fears losing the trust and confidence of an equal.

Style

Methods of Analyzing Style

The French novelist Stendhal defined style as follows: "Style consists in adding to a given thought all the circumstances calculated to produce the whole effect that the thought ought to produce." Since it is difficult to reach universal agreement on the "whole effect" that every idea ought to produce, it is much easier to cite stylistic characteristics of a given work than it is to reach agreement on the absolute merit of a particular style. Under the general heading of style one may list numerous characteristics, among which the following are the most notable: point of view, diction, imagery, arrangement (of sentences, paragraphs, chapters, sections), tone, mood or atmosphere, figurative language, rhythm, and pattern. Clearly, problems of style overlap with other considerations of the novel and cannot possibly be considered as separate entities. For example, if the reader speaks of the diction (choice of words) of one character as opposed to another, he is not only describing an aspect of style: he is also discussing characterization. Moreover, while the section on "Structure" considers foreshadowing and juxtaposition, those elements of fiction could well have been considered as aspects of style also.

1. Point of View

When applied to fiction, point of view does *not* mean an attitude held by the author. It means the angle of vision from which the narration is delivered. To determine the point of view and its significance for defining meaning, the reader should ask the following questions:

A. Who is the narrator? Is the narrator also the protagonist? the antagonist? a minor figure? simply an undramatized voice which does not exist as a character?

B. Does the narrator relate in the first or third person? Is the narrator *omniscient* (knows all, including motivation of characters)? Is the narrator *limited* (by geographical position, intelligence, bias, etc.)?

C. Is the novel related in a third-person dramatic point of view? This is the case when the narrator functions as a camera with sound track; that is, he describes the action and relays dialogue — but *does not interpret* actions or dialogue and does not enter the minds of the characters.

D. From what point in time does the narrator relate? Does he narrate at the same time as the events related? years after events which have been related to him by another?

E. How inclusive does the narrator consider his function to be? Does he simply relate events? judge events by established standards? generalize the significance of particular or related groups of events?

F. Are the narrator's observations and judgments reliable? If not, what aspect of his character or position most prominently leads to his unreliability?

2. Diction

A writer's diction is his choice of words in expressing ideas or emotions. If the layman reads a medical text or an advanced mathematics text, he will probably be weighed down by the fact that the author's profession has prescribed a diction which is to other men largely incomprehensible. The novelist, of course, is addressing a more mixed group of readers, but his choice of words is also dictated by his background or by certain conscious effects which he hopes to create. If the reader refuses to master the vocabulary of whaling, he cannot read *Moby-Dick*. The same is true of military diction in John Knowles' *A Separate Peace* and the diction of English lower classes in Daniel Defoe's *Moll Flanders*. At its simplest level, analysis of diction requires noting the particular profession, locale, age, or interest from which words are drawn.

An equally important task requires noting whether diction is *general* or *concrete* — that is, whether it creates a quite specific or a general image for the reader. Compare the following descriptions of a common subject: (1) "Mary is an incredibly ugly girl;" (2) "Mary weighs three hundred pounds. Her straggly hair stuck by perspiration to her unwashed face, she lumbered to the mirror. There she viewed her few yellowed teeth, the uneven scar which transversed her left cheek, and the infected redness from yesterday's squeezed pimples." Whereas general diction usually appeals to abstract mental concepts, concrete diction appeals to the bodily senses (sight, taste, etc.) and thus offers the reader a clearer sense of what the novelist means.

Diction may also be judged relative to its degree of formality or informality. The diction of Mark Twain's *Huck Finn,* for example, is very informal, using the idiom of an uneducated Southern boy; the diction of Henry James' *The Ambassadors,* on the other hand, is quite formal. A subcategory of formal diction includes foreign expressions and also allusions which would be unrecognized by certain readers (for example, allusions to Scripture, Shakespeare, classical mythology, etc.).

After preparing himself to describe the kinds of diction in a novel, the reader must question the novelist's effectiveness in his use of his diction. Various levels of diction may be employed to reveal distinctions in culture, education, and refinement of characters. On the other hand, they may be used because the author wishes a certain section of his work to be vividly concrete and another unclear and mysterious. In any case, the reader who would evaluate style must ask himself these questions.

3. Imagery

The term "image" denotes a particular and concrete detail in an artistic work which appeals to the reader's senses so strongly as to elicit a greater response than would the same detail in an everyday context. There are six common types of images: visual, auditory (sound), tactile (touch), gustatory (taste), olfactory (smell), and kinetic (movement). If throughout the novel a certain image is associated with a particular abstract idea (for example, the visual image black with evil or the auditory image of a vulture's cry with persecution or death), that image — because of the force it has on the reader's consciousness — has become a symbol. If there are a number of such relationships at work in the novel, one can speak of *patterns of imagery* or *patterns of symbolism*.

4. Mood or Atmosphere

The terms "mood" or "atmosphere" are general; they imply not a particular aspect of the novel but a prevailing emotional response which a part or the whole of the novel will generate. A reader may respond emotionally to a setting, a character, or an event in numerous ways: disgust, horror, fear, a sense of the grotesque, a sense of the ludicrous, etc.

A common mistake is the interchangeable use of these terms with either the term "tone" or "intent" or "intention." "Tone" denotes the author's attitude toward his subject; thus one may speak of tone as tragic, comic, melodramatic, ironic, etc. "Intent" or "intention" denotes the author's purpose. When Jonathan Swift in "A Modest Proposal" suggests that overpopulation and food shortage in Ireland could be solved by eating children, his tone is ironic and his intention satiric. The mood or atmosphere, on the other hand, is one of horror or of the grotesque.

5. Comparisons of Style

The reader must remember that point of view, figurative language, imagery, and other elements of style do not represent style itself. An author's style is his particular and unique combination of all of these elements. To generalize from similarities of one or more elements that two novels are stylistically comparable is extremely dangerous. For example, note the similarities in two such dissimilar works as *Huckleberry Finn* and *Great Expectations*: both are narrated in the first person; both build suspense by having a young boy help a person of another class (Magwitch and the Negro Jim) and then suffer pangs of conscience; both protagonists are virtually orphans who suffer at the hands of "civilized" society; both have protagonists who act in ignorance of significant details (Magwitch as the source of Pip's expectations and Tom Sawyer's knowing that Jim is already free); both protagonists are confronted by hypocritical and malicious characters; both protagonists try to execute the escape of a hidden criminal on a body of water; and both protagonists are forced at the end of the novel to accept a compromise of their original ideal of living. A cursory glance, however, will reveal that there are only surface similarities in the two novels; stylistically, they are quite opposed.

Chart: Methods of Revealing Character

	IMAGERY	DICTION	FIGURATIVE LANGUAGE
Joe	Associated with images of light, white, and heat.	Vocabulary largely substandard, though on occasions this realistic device is sacrificed. Since he is not happy conversing with a different social class, he tends to qualify statements so that little which is intelligible remains.	Having difficulty with literal expression, he never employs figurative language.
Miss Havisham	Associated with images of yellow, decay, and wailing sounds.	Language varies from harshness (in commands to Estella) to pitiful laments (in final scene with Pip).	Satis House itself is presented as a metaphor for her; both are decayed and crumbling for lack of admitting the healing light of day.
Estella	Associated with images of brightness, beauty, and hardness.	When she first meets Pip, her language is harsh and cruel. Later, though she lures him, her language remains concrete and lacking any terms for emotion.	Associates herself with inanimate objects; she must be "bent" into a better shape.

Jaggers	Uses strictly literal expression.	Vocabulary largely drawn from legal terminology. Also the diction is affected by his desire to remain uncommitted; thus there occurs the language of hypothetical situations and of propositions.	Associated with images of strength and hardness.
Wemmick	In Pip's opinion, he considers Jaggers' clients plants in a garden which he must keep.	With an emphasis on "portable property," he also uses a language of qualification and of legal origin.	Associated at office with images of hardness and of dustiness; at home with pastoral and heroic images.
Orlick	Associated with lurking animals of prey.	While merely substandard, his language suggests animal and guttural sounds.	Lurking, usually appears in darkness; associated with the marshland where he lives.
Wopsle	Comically associated with the dramatic roles he portrays.	In dialogue, he employs an elevated euphuistic vocabulary which suggests the egomaniac he is.	Associated with heroic figures (by which he is comically deflated).
Magwitch	Both as a young boy and as a man, Pip employs metaphors which associate Magwitch with both dogs and pursued animals.	Vocabulary largely substandard; in first appearance his physical state prescribes a preponderance of monosyllables.	Associated with images of darkness, persecution, and injustice.

Questions and Answers on Style

Question 11.

Describe the mode and significance of narrative point of view in *Great Expectations.*

Answer

Great Expectations is narrated in the first person by the novel's protagonist. A middle-aged, semi-educated partner in a moderately successful business, Philip Pirrip relates in the past tense the principal events, characters, and motives which filled his life from the age of seven to thirty-four (Pip is twenty-three when Magwitch returns; his return from business assignment abroad and meeting of Estella take place eleven years later). Although he relates actions completed in the past, the narrator's implied knowledge of the outcome of each confrontation he relates does not make him omniscient; he still finds the motives of his youth at times either ambiguous or mysterious. Moreover, the diction characterizing the narration reveals that he is only occasionally the intent critic who would analyze his youth. On more numerous occasions, the diction of the narration (as opposed to recounted dialogue) is that of a much younger man; in other words, he recalls a certain period in youth and consciously or unconsciously relates by employing only the facts, vocabulary, and intentions which were his at that particular time.

The double vision of the narrator (i.e., "I" the younger man and "I" the middle-aged businessman) and his narrating of events in chronological sequence make the tone of the novel unstable. Because the older narrator Pip provides the reader with hints and judgments which suggest the unreliability of the younger narrator, the reader consistently senses the outcome of situations before the protagonist does — thus establishing an ironic tone. However, the tone is not stable because the reader is also aware that his accurate estimation of the future only exceeds the protagonist's because of assistance derived from the older narrator. For example, long before Magwitch reappears the reader senses both that Magwitch is Pip's benefactor and that Miss Havisham is not — but on what evidence? Only two definite indications of Magwitch's gratitude and devotion appear while Pip is a very young boy: the captured Magwitch says he stole the food from Joe and later a man with the file brings a small monetary gift. The knowledge that Jaggers normally is associated with criminals could not aid Pip — for the lawyer demonstrably served Miss Havisham. On the other hand, judgments of other characters (Pumblechook, Mrs. Joe, and Herbert), chance circumstance (Jaggers' being both Pip's guardian and Miss Havisham's lawyer), and Miss Havisham's treachery all would — admittedly with little evidence — lead Pip to assume Miss

Havisham to be his benefactress. Significantly, though Herbert warns Pip of Miss Havisham's revenge plot and of the danger of Estella, he nevertheless also believes that she is Pip's benefactress.

Question 12.
Cite a particular pattern of imagery and discuss its effect in the development of the novel.

Answer
The most frequently recurring patterns of imagery throughout *Great Expectations* are the contrasting images of light or whiteness and dark or blackness. Images of light usually suggest growing perception, truth, and goodness, while images of black suggest ambiguity, falsity, and evil. The novel opens in the oppressive mist of approaching evening on the marshes. There Magwitch, dressed in coarse gray and covered with mud, approaches Pip and — together with the prevailing atmosphere — brings the boy to his first "vivid and broad impression of the identity of things." As the criminal leaves, Pip looks toward him and sees in the far distance "two black things:" a beacon by which sailors steer and a post where criminals were hanged and then left for public display. The black beacon, suggesting the extinguished hope of clarity, and the post, suggesting evil and persecution, foreshadow the delusion and suffering which will characterize Pip's life. Later, during the soldiers' pursuit of the two criminals in the marshes, there is a bitter sleet and torches are lit to penetrate the blackness. When Magwitch is captured, Pip views him by the light of the torches. Though the criminal lies to protect him and issues a sob which suggests the degree to which he has been moved by Pip's act of charity, Pip sees only the "black Hulk" which suggests that it is "all over with" the criminal. The fact that he does not sense Magwitch's emotion — thus would never suspect from Magwitch a reward for his act — is suggested by Pip's return to darkness after "the torches were flung hissing into the water."

Most vividly contrasted are the images associated with the forge and those with Satis House. Barricaded from the outside world, Satis House is faded like the woman who inhabits it. Led up the dark stairs by Estella (just as he will be led astray into the maze which will characterize his life), Pip notes the candle she carries as they approach Miss Havisham's room. Miss Havisham appears to be dressed in white (and for years Pip thinks of her as a good fairy godmother), but a closer observation reveals that all is not what it seemed initially: "Everything within my view which ought to be white, had been white long ago, and had lost its lustre, and was faded and yellow." Denying the light of day and living in a "yellowed" world, Miss Havisham will not radiate pure light until her dress is burned away by the redemptive fire. Joe, blond and associated with the fire of the forge, is exactly antithetical. An aura radiates about him as Pip notes when years later the blacksmith cares for him during his illness. Joe fights and easily defeats the black Orlick, who comes from the dismal sluice-house in the swamps, the place where he later attempts murder.

Magwitch's reappearance, and its providing Pip with a perception of the delusions which he has held, are emphasized by the criminal's walking up the darkened steps (under which Orlick hides) into Pip's room where a single light burns. Recalling his aiding the criminal, the proud Pip resents "the sort of bright and gratified recognition" that appears on Magwitch's face. Only after Pip commits himself, rejects the pose he has adopted, and makes his own life does the evening mist rise (as the morning mist had "solemnly risen" when he first left the forge) and permit a "broad expanse of tranquil light" to indicate that he will not again part with Estella.

Question 13.

To what extent does Dickens employ diction as a device for characterization in *Great Expectations?*

Answer

With few exceptions, both major and minor characters in *Great Expectations* are provided with unique diction and verbal patterns. Usually in each character's speech a particular phrase recurs which either suggests or epitomizes his social position, or clarifies the values which he upholds. Dickens' employment of a verbal signature for individual characters together with his tendency to associate individual bodily mannerisms with particular characters are two of the principal reasons that he is considered the greatest "character author" in English.

The clearest verbal signatures appear in the speech of either ill-educated or flat characters. No one, for example, could fail to identify Mrs. Joe's two favorite expressions: "I may truly say I've never had this apron of mine off" and "be grateful to them which brought you up by hand." The two expressions epitomize her pleasure in playing the role of the self-sacrificing and unappreciated martyr. Moreover, her preference for Pumblechook is reinforced on the level of diction; each of them is unconsciously redundant and each, when addressing the other, falls into a ritualized language that carries little more meaning than their mutual admiration. When dealing with social superiors, Pumblechook replaces his worldly and overbearing diction by a servile mode of expression which emphasizes his character as a "toady." His flattering manner is epitomized in the scene with Pip in which he repeatedly grasps his hand and says: "May I? — May I?" Wopsle's diction distinguishes him for his egomania, and takes the form of honoring nothing except lofty expressions which he himself utters. His reaction to the hissing of the audience which witnesses his grotesque portrayal of Hamlet suggests both his inclination toward falsely inflated diction and the blindness resulting from it: "My view is a little classic and thoughtful for them here; but they will improve, they will improve."

The diction of more prominent characters is equally individualized. Joe's expression, "which I meantersay," not only suggests his educational and social position; it also emphasizes that he is a man of action rather than words. Neither of his visits to Miss Havisham nor his visit to Pip's quarters in London comes of his own will. Uncomfortable with those higher on the social scale, language consistently fails him, thus motivating the qualifying clause "which I meantersay." Joe's eloquence (though Dickens at times provides him with unrealistically mature phrasing) is generally an eloquence in spite of language. The two-sided nature of Magwitch-Provis is also emphasized by totally contrasting patterns of diction. As Magwitch, his language is forceful — almost brutal; it suggests the strength which motivated his pursuit of wealth and his pursuit of Compeyson. An example of this is his stating of the less noble purpose for becoming Pip's benefactor: "If I ain't a gentleman, nor yet ain't got no learning, I'm the owner of such." As Provis, his language is humble and, as in his rhythmical references to Pip as "dear boy" and in his promises that he "ain't going to be low," implies a deep devotion to Pip and a pathetic desire not to disgrace himself in the eyes of the one person who ever displayed charity toward him. The diction of both Pip and Miss Havisham alters to reflect changes in allegiance. A frightened boy, a dissatisfied boy with growing social affectations, a snob, a disillusioned man, a hardworking successful businessman: these are the stages through which Pip moves, and each of the stages either offers or prescribes patterns of diction which Pip accepts. Most distinctive of all is the diction of Wemmick and Jaggers. In their office life, the language of law prevails. It includes numerous qualifying statements, the tendency to provide proposals or alternate questions instead of answering direct questions, and the ability to judge emphatically or withhold judgment altogether. The recurrence of the term "portable property" in Wemmick's speech is hardly more frequent than references to "evidence" in that of Jaggers.

*The Theme of Social Injustice in *Great Expectations*

I

On the surface *Great Expectations* is simply another very good example of that perennial *genre,* the education novel. In particular, it is the story of a restless young boy from the lower classes who comes into possession of a fortune he has done nothing to earn, founds a host of romantic aspirations upon it at the cost of becoming a snob, comes to be disappointed both romantically and socially, and, finally, with a more mature knowledge of himself and the world, works out his regeneration. As such, the novel is what G. K. Chesterton once called it, "an extra chapter to 'The Book of Snobs.' " But while admitting that Pip is a fairly good specimen of a certain type of mentality so dear to Dickens' satirical spirit, we cannot overlook the fact that Dickens is using his character to reveal some still more complex truths about society and its organization.

Though its shorter length and more compact organization have prevented it from being classed with *Bleak House, Little Dorrit,* and *Our Mutual Friend, Great Expectations* is really of a piece with that great social "trilogy" of Dickens' later years. In the briefer novel Dickens is attempting only a slightly less comprehensive anatomization of social evil; thematically, the implications of Pip's story are almost as large. Consider, for instance, how many different strata of society are gotten into the comparatively small number of pages that story takes up. In the first six chapters alone we meet members of the criminal, the military, and the artisan classes, together with a parish clerk and two well-to-do entrepreneurs. The principal difference between *Great Expectations* and the more massive panoramic novels lies more in the artistic means employed than in the intellectual content. In *Great Expectations* Dickens strips the larger novels to their intellectual essentials. The point of one line of action in *Bleak House,* we remember, was to show how Lady Dedlock had been victimized by social injustice operating in the form of conventional morality and its hypocrisies. But into that novel Dickens also packed a great deal else; the Lady Dedlock action was but part of a gigantic network. In *Great Expectations* all such additional ramifications are discarded. Dickens concentrates with great intensity upon a single line of development, and, to our suprise, this line turns out to be remarkably similar in its theme to that of Lady Dedlock's story. For Pip's career shows not only a hapless young man duped by his poor illusions, but a late victim in a long chain of widespread social injustice.

*By John H. Hagen, Jr. *Nineteenth Century Fiction,* IX, 3(December, 1954).

The story's essential features make this fact plain. We learn in Chapter 42 that the prime mover, so to speak, of the entire course of events which the novel treats immediately or in retrospect is a man by the name of Compeyson, a cad who adopts the airs of a "gentleman." Significantly, he remains throughout the book shrouded in mist (literal and figurative), vague, remote, and terrifying, like some vast impersonal force. Through his actions two people once came to grief. First, after stripping her of a great deal of her fortune, he jilted the spoiled and naïve Miss Havisham, and thereby turned her wits against the whole male sex. Secondly, he further corrupted a man named Magwitch who had already been injured by poverty, and revealed to him how easily the law may be twisted into an instrument of class. The trial of Magwitch and Compeyson is so important a key to the novel's larger meanings that the former's description of it in the later pages of the book should be read in entirety. What the passage reveals is that impartiality in the courts is often a myth. Judges and jury alike may be swayed by class prejudice. The whole judicial system may tend to perpetuate class antagonism and hostility. In short, an important element at the root of Magwitch's career is great social evil: the evil of poverty, and the evil of a corruptible judicial system. Though not entirely so, Magwitch is certainly, in part, a victim. The conventional words Pip speaks over his corpse at the end —" 'O Lord, be merciful to him a sinner' "— remain merely conventional, for the man was more sinned against than sinning. From his very first appearance in the novel, when we see him shivering on the icy marshes, he is depicted with sympathy, and by the time we get to the end, he has risen to an almost heroic dignity.

The connection of all this with Pip is plain. The young boy becomes for both Magwitch and Miss Havisham a means by which, in their different ways, they can retaliate against the society that injured them. One of Miss Havisham's objects is, through Pip, to frustrate her greedy relatives who, like Compeyson himself, are interested in her for her money alone, and who, again like Compeyson, typify the rapacious and predatory elements of society at large. Magwitch, on the other hand, retaliates against society by striving to meet it on the ground of its own special prejudices. Though deprived from childhood of the opportunity to become a "gentleman" himself, he does not vow destruction to the "gentleman" class. Having seen in Compeyson the power of that class, the deference it receives from society, he fashions a gentleman of his own to take his place in it. He is satisfied to live vicariously through Pip, to show society that he can come up to its standards, and, by raising his pawn into the inner circle, to prove that it is no longer impregnable.

Thus Pip, in becoming the focal point for Miss Havisham's and Magwitch's retaliation — the one who is caught in the midst of the cross fire directed against society by two of the parties it injured, who, in turn, display in their desire for proprietorship some of the very tyranny and selfishness against which they are rebelling — becomes society's scapegoat. It is he who must pay the price for original outrages against justice, who must suffer for the wider injustices of the whole society of which he is but a humble part. The result is that he too takes on society's vices, its selfishness, ingratitude, extravagance, and pride. He, too, becomes something of an impostor like Compeyson himself, and thereby follows in the fatal footsteps of the very man who is indirectly the cause of his future misery. Thus the worst qualities of society seem inevitably to propagate themselves in a kind of vicious circle. Paralleling the case of Pip is that of Estella. As Pip is the creation of Magwitch, she is the creation of Miss Havisham. Her perversion has started earlier; as the novel opens, it is Pip's turn next. He is to be the latest heir of original injustice, the next to fall victim to the distortions that have already been forced upon Magwitch, Miss Havisham, and Estella. He is to be the latest product of Compeyson's evil as it continues to infect life.

But injustice does not come to bear upon Pip through Magwitch and Miss Havisham alone. There is injustice under the roof of his own house. Throughout the first stage of Pip's career, Dickens presents dramatically in scene after scene the petty tyranny exercised over the boy by his shrewish sister, Mrs. Gargery, and some of her friends, particularly Mr. Pumblechook, the blustering corn merchant, and Wopsle, the theatrically-minded parish clerk. It is the constant goading Pip receives from these people that makes him peculiarly susceptible to the lure of his "great expectations" with their promise of escape and freedom. But more important is the fact that it is Pumblechook and Mrs. Gargery who first put the treacherous idea into Pip's head that Miss Havisham is his secret patroness. One of the very reasons they insist upon his waiting on the old woman in the first place is their belief that she will liberally reward him, and thereafter they never let the idea out of the boy's mind. In short, Mrs. Gargery, Pumblechook, and Wopsle do as much as Magwitch and Miss Havisham to turn Pip into his erring ways. To be sure, the novel is not an essay in determinism. But despite the legitimacy of the reproaches of Pip's conscience, we cannot forget how early his impressionable mind was stamped with the images of greed and injustice — images that present a small-scale version of the greedy and unjust world of "respectability" as a whole. The tyranny exercised over Pip by his sister, Pumblechook, and their like is a type of the tyranny exercised by the conventionally "superior" elements of society over the suffering and dispossessed. Theirs is a version of the greedy and unjust world of "respectability" as a whole. The dunghills in which Magwitch and his kind are spawned, and then throws such men into chains when they violate the law. When

Pumblechook boasts of himself as the instrument of Pip's wealth, he is truthful in a way he never suspects or would care to suspect. For the obsequious attitude toward money he exemplifies is, indirectly, at the root of Pip's new fortune. It was just such an attitude that resulted in the debasing of Magwitch below Compeyson at their trial, and thus resulted in the former's fatal determination to transform Pip into a "gentleman."

Injustice is thus at the heart of the matter — injustice working upon and through the elders of Pip and Estella, and continuing its reign in the children themselves. With these children, therefore, we have a theme analogous to one deeply pondered by another great Victorian novelist: the idea of "consequences" as developed by George Eliot. Both she and Dickens are moved by a terrifying vision of the wide extent to which pollution can penetrate the different, apparently separate and unrelated, members of society. Once an act of injustice has been committed, there is no predicting to what extent it will affect the lives of generations yet unborn and of people far removed in the social scale from the victims of the original oppression. Though on a smaller scale, Dickens succeeds no less in *Great Expectations* than in his larger panoramic novels in suggesting a comprehensive social situation. No less than in *Bleak House, Little Dorrit,* and *Our Mutual Friend* — and in *A Tale of Two Cities* as well — the different levels of society are brought together in a web of sin, injustice, crime, and destruction. The scheme bears an analogy to the hereditary diseases running throughout several generations in Zola's *Les Rougons-Macquarts* series. Dickens compresses his material more than Zola by starting *in medias res,* and showing Pip as the focal point for the past, present, and future at once. In him are concentrated the effects of previous injustice, and he holds in himself the injustice yet to come. The interest of the novel is never restricted merely to the present. Dickens opens a great vista, a "poor labyrinth," through which we may see the present as but the culmination of a long history of social evil. Society is never able to smother wholly the facts of its injustice. As Dickens shows in novel after novel, somehow these facts will come to light again: Bounderby's mother in *Hard Times* rises to reveal her sons' hypocrisy to the crowd he has bullied for so many years; the facts of Mrs. Clennam's relationship to the Dorrit family, and of society's injury to Lady Dedlock, her lover, and her child, are all unearthed in the end. Immediate victims may be skillfully suppressed, as Magwitch, returning from exile, is finally caught and imprisoned again. But the baleful effects of social evil go on in a kind of incalculable chain reaction. It is the old theme of tragic drama read into the bleak world of Mid-Victorian England: the sins of the fathers will be visited upon the heads of their children; the curse on the house will have to be expiated by future generations of sufferers.

Thus it is fair to say that Pip's story is more than a study of personal development. In his lonely struggle to work out his salvation, he is atoning for the guilt of society at large. In learning to rise above selfishness, to attain to a selfless love for Magwitch, he brings to an end the chain of evil that was first forged by the selfish Compeyson. His regeneration has something of the same force as Krook's "spontaneous combustion" in *Bleak House,* or the collapse of the Clennam mansion in *Little Dorrit,* or even the renunciation of his family heritage by Charles Darnay in *A Tale of Two Cities.* Just as Darnay must atone for the guilt of his family by renouncing his property, so Pip must atone for the evils of the society that has corrupted him by relinquishing his unearned wealth. And as Darnay marries the girl whose father was one of the victims of his family's oppression, so Pip desires to marry the girl whose father, Magwitch, is the victim of the very society whose values Pip himself has embraced.

II

In giving his theme imaginative embodiment Dickens used what are perhaps some of the most ingenious and successful devices of his entire career. With disarming suddenness, for example, *Great Expectations* opens with the presentation of a physical phenomenon almost as memorable as that of the fog in *Bleak House*: the marshes. More than a Gothic detail casually introduced to give the story an eerie beginning, the marshes reappear again and again, not only in the first six chapters, where indeed they figure most prominently, but throughout the book. They haunt the novel from start to finish, becoming finally one of its great informing symbols. The variety of ways in which Dickens manages unobtrusively to weave them, almost like a musical motif, into the texture of his tale is remarkable. At one time they may flicker briefly across the foreground of one of Pip's casual reveries; at another they may provide the material of a simile; or Pip may return to them in fact when he is summoned there late in the story by Orlick; or, again, he may see them from a distance when he is helping Magwitch make his getaway down the Thames. "It was like my own marsh country," Pip says of the landscape along the part of the river he and Magwitch traverse:

. . . some ballast lighters, shaped like a child's first rude imitation of a boat, lay low in the mud; and a little squat shoal-lighthouse on open piles, stood crippled in the mud on stilts and crutches: and slimy stakes stuck out of the mud, and slimy stones stuck out of the mud, and red landmarks and tidemarks stuck out of the mud, and an old landing-stage and an old roofless building slipped into the mud, and all about us was stagnation and mud.

Mud is a peculiarly appropriate symbol for the class of society that Magwitch represents — the downtrodden and oppressed of life, all those victims of injustice whom society has tried to submerge. It is a natural image of the social dunghill in which violence and rebellion are fomented, the breeding place of death. Likewise, it is the condition of death itself upon which certain forms of life must feed. It is no accident on Dickens' part that when Pip and his companions stop at a public house on their journey down the river, they meet a "slimy and smeary" dock attendant whose clothes have all been taken from the bodies of drowned men. In fact, the motif of life thriving upon death is underlined more than once throughout the novel in a number of small but brilliant ways. On his first trip to Newgate, Pip meets a man wearing "mildewed clothes, which had evidently not belonged to him originally, and which, I took it into my head, he had bought cheap of the executioner." Trabb, the haberdasher and funeral director of Pip's village, is still another kind of scavenger. He, too, like the many undertakers in Dickens' other novels and Mrs. Gamp in *Martin Chuzzlewit*, profits hideously by the misfortunes of others. It is this condition that Dickens sums up most effectively in the repulsive image of mud.

But together with the marshes, he uses still another symbol to keep the idea of social injustice and its consequences before us. Chapter I opens with a description of the graveyard in which Pip's parents and several infant brothers are buried. Though less prominent as an image than the marshes, that of the grave presents much more explicitly the idea of the death-in-life state to which Magwitch and others in his predicament are condemned. We remember that it is from among the tombstones that Magwitch first leaps forth into the story; and when, at the end of the chapter, he is going away, Pip has been so impressed by his likeness to a risen corpse that he imagines the occupants of the graveyard reaching forth to reclaim him. This is not a merely facetious or lurid detail. The grave imagery suggests in a highly imaginative way the novel's basic situation. Magwitch, in relation to the "respectable" orders of society, is dead; immured in the Hulks or transported to the fringes of civilization, he is temporarily removed from active life. But when in the opening scene of the book he rises from behind the tombstone, he is figuratively coming back to life again, and we are witnessing the recurrence of an idea Dickens made a central motif of *A Tale of Two Cities,* the idea of resurrection and revolution. When Magwitch looms up from the darkened stairwell of Pip's London lodging house at the end of the second stage of the boy's career, we are witnessing, as in the case of Dr. Manette's being "recalled to life" from the Bastille, an event of revolutionary implications. For what this means is that one whom society has tried to repress, to shut out of life, has refused to submit to the edict. He has come back to take his place once more in the affairs of men, and to influence them openly in a decisive way. The injuries society perpetrates on certain of its members will be thrust back upon it. Society, like an individual, cannot escape the consequences of its injustice; an evil or an injury once done continues to infect and poison life, to pollute the society responsible for it.

This is suggested by the very way in which the material of the novel is laid out. Within the first six chapters, Dickens regularly alternates outdoor and indoor scenes, each one of which is coincident with a chapter division. There is a steady movement back and forth between the shelter and warmth of the Gargery's house and the cold misery and danger of the marshes. Thus, while getting his plot under way, Dickens is at the same time vividly impressing upon us his fundamental idea of two worlds: the world of "respectability" and the world of ignominy; of oppressors and of oppressed; of the living and of the dead. In the first six chapters these worlds are separate; it is necessary to come in or to go out in order to get from either one to the other. But in his excursions from the house to the marshes and back again, Pip is already forging the link that is to bring them together at the end of the second stage of his adventures when Magwitch, refusing to be left out in the cold any longer, actually becomes an inhabitant of Pip's private rooms. The clearest hint of this coming revolution is given when the soldiers burst from the marshes into Joe's house, and disrupt the solemn Christmas dinner. The breaking in upon it of the forces of another world shows on what a sandy foundation the complacency of Pumblechook and his kind is based. Beneath the self-assured crust of society, the elements of discontent and rebellion are continually seething, continually threatening to erupt. Thus the alternation between worlds that gives the novel's first six chapters their order supplies the reader at once with the basic moral of the book as a whole: the victims of injustice cannot be shut out of life forever; sooner or later they will come into violent contact with their oppressors.

Moving from the early pages of the book to the larger pattern, we discover that alternation between two different locales is basic to the whole. Pip tries to make his home in London, but he is forced a number of times to return to the site of his former life, and each return brings him a new insight into the truth of his position, one progressively more severe than another. The alternation between London and the old village becomes for Dickens a means of suggesting what the alternation between outdoor and indoor scenes in the first six chapters suggested: pretend as one will, reality will eventually shatter the veil of self-deception. Like the individual who has come to sacrifice his integrity for society's false values only to find it impossible to deny indefinitely his origins and the reality upon which his condition rests, society cannot effectively stifle all the victims of its injustice and oppression. There will always be men like Jaggers — men to connect the dead with the living, to act as the link between the underground man and the rest of society. As a defender of criminals, Jaggers is the great flaw in society's repression of its victims; he is their hope of salvation and resurrection. Like Tulkinghorn, the attorney in *Bleak House,* he knows everybody's secrets; he is the man to whom the lines between the high and the low, the men of property and the dispossessed, are no barrier. A wise and disillusioned Olympian, Jaggers comments like a tragic chorus on the two great worlds that are the product and expression of social injustice, for the existence of which Pip and others must suffer the terrible consequences.

*The Hero in *Great Expectations*

My first most vivid and broad impression of the identity of things, seems to me to have been gained on a memorable raw afternoon towards evening. At such a time I found out for certain, that this bleak place overgrown with nettles was the churchyard; and that Philip Pirrip, late of this parish, and also Georgiana wife of the above, were dead and buried; and that Alexander, Bartholomew, Abraham, Tobias, and Roger, infant children of the aforesaid, were also dead and buried; and that the dark flat wilderness beyond the churchyard, intersected with dykes and mounds and gates, with scattered cattle feeding on it, was the marshes; and that the low leaden line beyond was the river; and that the distant savage lair from which the wind was rushing, was the sea; and that the small bundle of shivers growing afraid of it all and beginning to cry, was Pip.(1)[1]

Great Expectations is the most unified and concentrated expression of Dickens' abiding sense of the world, and Pip might be called the archetypal Dickens hero. In *Great Expectations* Dickens' particular view of things is expressed with a concreteness and symbolic intensity he never surpassed. Perhaps the restrictions of shorter length and of weekly rather than monthly publication led Dickens to present his story more in symbolic than in discursive form. The result is not a narrowing and rarefying of meaning, but rather a large increase in intensity and complexity. What it took Dickens in 1850 the first hundred pages of *David Copperfield* to say is presented far more powerfully in the first few pages of *Great Expectations*: the lonely boy becoming aware of his desolation on the dark marshes in the midst of a hostile universe, standing by the graves of his mother, father, and brothers, aware that he will be beaten by his foster mother when he returns home, and suddenly ter-

*(Editor's title) By J. Hillis Miller. From *Charles Dickens: the World of His Novels,* Harvard University Press, 1958.
[1]Numbers in parentheses refer to chapters in *Great Expectations*.

141

rified by the apparition of the "fearful man""'starting up from among the graves"(1). What had been presented seriatim in the earlier novels is here said with poetic compression. And in following Pip's adventures we perhaps come closest to the intimate center of Dickens' apprehension of the world and of his mode of existence within it. *Great Expectations* makes available, as does no other of Dickens' novels, the central experiences of the universal Dickensian hero.

Never, perhaps, was the form of a great novel conceived as the response to so practical a demand. In the early fall of 1860 the sales of *All the Year Round* were dropping sadly because of the unpopularity of Charles Lever's *The Day's Ride*. Dickens "dashed" in with *Great Expectations* in order to save circulation. At first *Great Expectations* was a "little piece." Then as the idea grew — "such a very fine, new, and grotesque idea" — it was planned as a monthly serial of twenty numbers, like *Bleak House* or *Little Dorrit*. Then, because of the falling-off of the sales of *All the Year Round,* Dickens decided to write it in the much briefer form of a serial in weekly numbers for that journal.

Dickens' own language for what he was doing scarcely reveals its importance. The central motif of *Great Expectations,* the *donnée* with which Dickens began, was the secret manipulation of Pip's life by Magwitch the convict — a striking idea, which goes to the roots of several key nineteenth-century notions about human existence. Dickens' phrase for it was "the grotesque tragi-comic conception that first encouraged me." We have only one important sign of the depths which Dickens was plumbing in the conception of the basic motif of *Great Expectations*: "To be quite sure I had fallen into no unconscious repetitions, I read David Copperfield again the other day, and was affected by it to a degree you would hardly believe." This is a valuable reinforcement of the sense we get from the novel itself that Dickens was here drawing again, as in *David Copperfield*, on his most intimate personal experiences. They are transformed into a "fable," perhaps, but still retain the essential form of Dickens' sense of the meaning of his own life.

What form does this meaning take?

Great Expectations, like most of Dickens' novels, does not begin with a description of the perfect bliss of childhood, the period when the world and the self are identified, and the parents are seen as benign gods whose care and whose overlooking judgment protect and justify the child. Like Oedipus, who, as a new born baby, was put out in the fields to die, Dickens' heroes and heroines have never experienced this perfect security. Each becomes aware of himself as isolated from all that is outside of himself. The Dickensian hero is separated from nature. The world appears to him as cold and unfriendly, as a "wilderness" or a graveyard. In Dickens there is no Wordsworthian theory of the child's filial bond with nature. There is no moment of primitive or infantile identification of subject and object, self and world, followed by a "fall" into the cruel realm of time and division. The self is not initially the plenitude of a union with the entire universe, but is already down to "the small bundle of shivers growing afraid of it all and beginning to cry." The Dickensian hero is also alienated from the human community. He has no familiar tie. He is an orphan, or illegitimate, or both. He has no status in the community, no inherited role which he can accept with dignity. He is characterized by desire, rather than by possession. His spiritual state is one of an expectation founded on a present consciousness of lack, of deprivation. He is, in Wallace Stevens' phrase, "an emptiness that would be filled."

Furthermore, the Dickensian hero becomes aware of himself as guilty. His very existence is a matter of reproach and a shameful thing. Esther Summerson's foster mother tells her that it would have been better if she had never been born, and Pip says of himself: "I was always treated as if I had insisted on being born in opposition to the dictates of reason, religion, and morality, and against the dissuading arguments of my best friends"(1). It is mere accident that he is alive at all, and is not buried beside his brothers in the lonely churchyard by the sea. "As to you," says Joe of his first glimpse of the infant Pip, "if you could have been aware how small and flabby and mean you was, dear me, you'd have formed the most contemptible opinions of yourself!"(7). And Mrs. Joe recalls "all the times she had wished |Pip| in |his| grave, and |he| had contumaciously refused to go there"(4). The typical Dickens hero, like Pip, feels guilty because he has no given status or relation to nature, to family, or to the community. He is, in everyone's eyes, in the way, superfluous. He is either ignored by society altogether, thrown into the streets to beg or starve, or he is taken care of by the state or by his foster parents in an impersonal way which deprives him of any real identity. To submit to this "care" is to be transformed into an object. He may, alternatively, accept a job as a functionary in the vast system of money-getting which dominates urban society. This will as effectively dehumanize him as going to the poorhouse. Dickens shows that, for his characters at least, no "natural right" exists, no "state" in the sense that Rousseau and Matthew Arnold meant it: something above all hereditary legitimacies and distinctions, something to which the individual may tie himself and submit, as to his own best self. For Dickens, such submission means to lose all one's specifically human qualities of self-consciousness and freedom. Submission to the collective process of making and selling, of "beggaring your neighbor" lest he "beggar" you, is to be in danger of becoming dehumanized, like Wemmick, who is "a dry man, . . . with a square wooden face, whose expression seem|s| to have been imperfectly chipped out with a dulledged chisel"(21). Or, even worse, the individual may be destroyed altogether by society, and remain behind only as the trophy of somebody's successful manipulations, like Jaggers' clients, who have been transformed into "dreadful casts on a shelf, of faces peculiarly swollen, and twitchy about the nose"(20).

Since the Dickensian hero has initially no real role, any status he attains in the world will be the result of his own efforts. He will be totally responsible, himself, for any identity he achieves, and thus "guilty" in the sense of being the source of his own values. He has no hope of ever being justified by any external approval. He will be, whatever he does, a "self-made man," a man who has made himself his own goal and end. This will be true in spite of any efforts on his part to escape his superfluity. The world has simply refused to give him any assigned place, and any place he gets will have to be seized.

Given such a situation, the hero can remove himself from the world in which he has no place, withdraw into a solitary enclosure. Suicide is not really an option for Dickens' characters, except for those who are completely evil, but withdrawal and passivity are possible. In different ways, for example, Arthur Clennam, Mrs. Clennam, John Harmon, and Miss Havisham attempt to escape from the threat of dehumanization by willing not to will, by abnegation, by a passive drifting which will, they vainly hope, relieve them of the guilt of action. On the other hand, the Dickensian hero can submit to the complete dehumanization which society or his stepparents would practice upon him, or, finally, he can take upon himself the responsibility and guilt of a selfhood which is to be made, not accepted from the outside. In one case, he tries to hide from himself his freedom by submitting to the role society would have him play. He thus becomes one of Dickens' comic automatons, like Wemmick, who at first seems to be a wooden puppet manipulated by external forces, wholly lacking in real human qualities, mouthing the dead language of cliché and slogan: "My guiding star," says Wemmick, "is: Get hold of Portable Property." In the other case, he consciously sets himself up as an end in himself. He is then in danger of becoming, like Blandois in *Little Dorrit,* a demonic individualist whose hand is against his neighbor, and who hopes to achieve personal identity by the destruction of everything that is. But Dickens' true heroes and heroines, those characters at the centers of his novels, seek some intermediary between these extremes. They seek some way out that will make possible the achievement of true selfhood, while not necessitating the extreme of anarchic individualism. These protagonists try various ways, some proper, some improper, of attaining the reconciliation of freedom and security. The single great development in Dickens' world view is the change in the kinds of expedients which are deemed to be proper or possible. *Great Expectations* is the novel in which the various alternatives are most clearly presented and opposed.

Bibliography

Carey, John. *The Violent Effigy*. London: Faber and Faber, 1979.

Chesterton, Gilbert Keith. *Charles Dickens*. New York: Schocken Books, 1965. (Originally published in London in 1906.)

Dyson, A. E. *The Inimitable Dickens*. London: Macmillan and Co. Ltd., 1970.

Engel, Monroe. *The Maturity of Dickens*. Cambridge, Massachusetts: Harvard University Press, 1959.

Fielding, K. J. *Charles Dickens: A Critical Introduction*. New York: David McKay Co., 1958.

Forster, John. *The Life of Charles Dickens,* 2 vols. New York: E. P. Dutton, 1928. (Published in London in three volumes, 1872-74.)

Gissing, George. *Critical Studies of the Works of Charles Dickens*. New York, Greenberg, 1924.

Haines, Charles. *Charles Dickens*. New York: Franklin Watts, Inc., 1969.

House, Humphry. *The Dickens World,* 2nd ed. New York: Oxford University Press, 1960.

Huxley, Aldous. *Vulgarity in Literature*. London: Chatto and Windus, 1930.

Johnson, Edgar, *Charles Dickens: His Tragedy and Triumph,* 2 vols. New York: Simon and Schuster, 1953. (The standard biography.)

Kaplan, Fred. *Dickens and Mesmerism*. Princeton: Princeton University Press, 1975.

Leacock, Stephen. *Charles Dickens: His Life and Work*. Garden City, New York: Doubleday, Doran, 1934.

Ley, J. W. T. *The Dickens Circle*. London: Chapman and Hall, 1919.

Miller, J. Hillis. *Charles Dickens: The World of His Novels*. Cambridge, Massachusetts: Harvard University Press, 1959.

Nisbet, Ada. *Dickens and Ellen Ternan*. Berkeley: University of California Press, 1952.

Orwell, George. *Dickens, Dali and Others*. New York: Harcourt, Brace, 1946.

Pearson, Hesketh. *Dickens: His Character, Comedy, and Career*. New York: Harper and Brothers, 1949.

Pope-Hennessy, Una. *Charles Dickens: 1812-1870*. London: Howell, Soskin, 1946.

Santayana, George. *Soliloquies in England*. London, 1922. (In *The Dial*.)

Van Ghent, Dorothy. *The English Novel: Form and Function*. New York: Holt, Rinehart and Winston, 1953.

Wilson, Edmund. *The Wound and the Bow*. New York: Oxford University Press, 1947.

NOTES